HERALDRY IN BRITAIN

A symbolic Crown and a simplified rendering of the Royal Arms, both designed by Milner Gray, R.D.I., F.S.I.A., for the Council of Industrial Design's Coronation Souvenirs Committee. The purpose is to help manufacturers and members of the public in their quest for appropriate emblems to reproduce by various processes in Coronation souvenirs, street decorations, displays and favours. The designs conform to all restrictions on the use of the Crown and Royal Arms.

HERALDRY
IN
BRITAIN

BY
GEORGE EVANS

W. & G. FOYLE LTD.
119-125, CHARING CROSS ROAD, LONDON, W.C.2

PUBLISHED IN THE U. S. A. BY
DOVER PUBLICATIONS, INC.
920 BROADWAY, NEW YORK 10, N. Y.

First Published 1953

PRINTED IN GREAT BRITAIN BY
EBENEZER BAYLIS AND SON, LTD., THE
TRINITY PRESS, WORCESTER, AND LONDON

CONTENTS

ACKNOWLEDGMENTS

I HAVE to thank the Most Honourable the Marquess of Cholmondele for permission to reproduce the Hatchment on the cover and in th text, and for reading the chapter on this subject in the manuscrip

To the Hon. Sir George Bellew, C.V.O., Garter King of Arm and Sir Thomas Innes of Learney, K.C.V.O., Lord Lyon King (Arms, my especial thanks are due for kindly reading and correctin that part of the manuscript relating to the Heralds and for permi sion to reproduce the arms of their office.

I am grateful also to the Secretary of the Chancery of the Order (St. Michael and St. George for his valuable information concern ing the Stalls, Banners and Stall Plates in St. Paul's Cathedral.

I am indebted to The Heraldry Society and Mr. Rowland Brettc for permission to reproduce Figs. 58 to 65 which appeared in th Society's quarterly Journal (The Coat of Arms) and to the Britis Broadcasting Corporation, The National Coal Board, Barclay Bank Ltd., Scottish Aviation Ltd., The Institution of Electric Engineers, and the Borough of Beckenham, for kindly supplyin illustrations of their arms, and to The Times and Controller of H.N Stationery Office for the illustrations of the Royal Arms.

Also to Mr. Gordon Eckett for his collaboration with the draw ings and for the photograph of the Hatchment used on the fro cover.

Finally, to Mrs. Jane Eckett, who has typed and re-typed th manuscript for me, I extend my very grateful thanks.

GEORGE EVAN

Beckenham,
Kent.
1952.

FOREWORD

HERALDRY is generally considered to be one of the more esoteric arts; comparable, say, to the study of Chaldaic manuscripts or the domestic habits of deep-sea fish. Yet there was a time when it was once "the pursuit and delight of every gentleman" and it is to be regretted that this is no longer the case. The growth of materialism, utilitarianism and a host of unlovely sciences is partly to blame for this falling off, but so also is the dearth of attractive, reasonably-priced guides to Heraldry. This excellent book should help greatly to remedy this deficiency.

Heraldry has a fascination all its own; it has its own language, its own arts and its own history. Those who condemn it as useless and out of date speak unwisely. At worst it is a splendid hobby and at best it stimulates legitimate pride in family, school, town, county and country, being symbolic of that unity and continuity, without which there can be no real progress, no real national life. It provides colour in a drab age and unites men more effectively and more permanently than a thousand political harangues.

This little book brings heraldry within the reach of all and I feel sure that none of those who pursue it will regret the day on which they started their pilgrimage, Mr. Evans's guide in hand, into a wonderland of colour and romance where bowler hats, outsized photographs of film stars and advertisements for baby-sitters are blissfully forgotten.

J. P. BROOKE-LITTLE,
Chairman of The Heraldry Society

East Knoyle,
Wiltshire.

THE ORIGIN AND GROWTH OF HERALDRY

"The boast of Heraldry, the pomp of Power"—Gray's Elegy.

THE term Heraldry, broadly speaking, is understood by most people to mean the display or description and authentication of Coats of Arms, whereas in actual fact it includes all that appertains to the duties of a Herald. The art of Heraldry is termed Armoury and the products of this form of creative art are termed Armorial Bearings.

The seventeenth century writers like Sylvannus Morgan wove a good deal of fantasy into their heraldic works, so we can safely ignore their statements on the pre-conquest origin of Heraldry, and accept on evidence only that it was not until the beginning of the twelfth century that Heraldry appeared.

The famous Bayeux Tapestry illustrates devices on shields and flags, but these do not conform to laws of Heraldry.

Having its origin in the tournaments of the feudal ages and receiving a tremendous impetus during the second Crusade, Heraldry assumed an exclusive and hereditary character which has since been maintained as its most distinctive attribute. The religious orders too, further increased its popularity by incorporating its devices in their monastic buildings and manuscripts.

Arms in the first instance were assumed without any formal grant, but later the King asserted his right to grant arms and throughout the Middle Ages grants were made personally by the Sovereign for services rendered and deeds of valour.

It is therefore not surprising that having obtained a coat of arms at considerable risk, the possession of such an award should be treasured by the recipient and his descendants.

It was also possible for an Armiger (one possessing a grant of arms by grant or heredity) to gain an augmentation for personal bravery or service to the King or country.

A striking example of this can be seen in the arms of the Duke of

Wellington (Fig. 1). This great soldier was permitted to surcharge his shield with an inescutcheon (smaller shield within the shield) bearing on it the Union Flag as a recognition for his services to the nation.

FIG. I. THE ARMS OF THE
DUKE OF WELLINGTON.

Heraldry or Armoury from its beginning was intended to serve a practical purpose. Originating in that Age of Chivalry when devices were essential to distinguish clearly the armoured knights both in the tournament lists as well as on the field of battle, the devices were also used on the Seals attached to documents as ready marks of identity. During the thirteenth century it became cus-

FIG. 2. SURCOAT
FROM THE EFFIGY OF
THE BLACK PRINCE'S
TOMB IN CANTERBURY
CATHEDRAL.

tomary to embroider the charges of the shield on a Surcoat (Fig. 2) and it is this practice which has given rise to the expression "Coat of Arms"; even to-day the Heralds can be seen at State Ceremonies clad in their coats of arms, or TABARDS. The very general use of arms in the early days caused confusion by the assumption of the same devices by various feudal lords, probably for the reason that so few devices were then in use. As Heraldry gained a greater hold, its claims were recognized and it became imperative to appoint some authority who in this matter should represent the Sovereign, and on his behalf make grants of arms, keeping records of those granted, settling disputes on the rights to bear arms, and disallowing all those which were not proved. To accomplish this, Heralds' Visitations were instituted in 1413 and were held at intervals of about thirty years down to 1686. From the records then made much valuable information can be obtained.

The College of Arms was established in 1484, and the duties of its Officers included the marshalling of all State functions, tournaments, etc.

FIG. 3.

THE ACHIEVEMENT OF THE
4TH MARQUESS OF CHOLMONDELEY.

As early as the reign of Edward I it became customary for women also to participate in the honour conferred by a coat of arms, married women adopting those of their husbands conjoined by impalement with the arms of their father (Fig. 3) and from the fifteenth century onwards, to further distinguish the arms of widows and spinsters, the arms were borne on a lozenge instead of a shield (Fig. 48). This ruling did not apply to the Queen as Sovereign.

Edward III was the first monarch to impress his arms on the coinage of the country, a custom which still survives. Having attained a high state of popularity and symbolizing as it did all that was great and chivalrous, it naturally followed that Heraldry entered very largely into all forms of decorative work. Buildings, both monastic and secular, furniture, fabrics, manuscripts, and even the wearing apparel for both man and horse, were made gay with heraldic devices.

Although much has been destroyed with the passage of time, much remains to remind us of the importance of Heraldry in the everyday life of the times, and it is of great interest to trace the development of this traditional art from its inception in the twelfth century through its various phases, good and bad, to the present day, when it may be said that the greater part of heraldic design, especially that now produced by or under the influence of the College of Arms, would be hard to match at any other period.

Some of the finest examples of modern Heraldry have been created by Mr. Hugh Easton in the new stained glass windows in Westminster Abbey commemorating, respectively the Battle of Britain (Henry VII Chapel), the Nursing Services (window over the Islip Chapel), and the new window for the Islip Chapel itself.

Two superb series in stone are the King's Beasts surmounting the pinnacles and buttresses of St. George's Chapel, Windsor (1925), and the Tudor Beasts on the moat bridge of Hampton Court (1909); while the enamelled stall plates of the members of the Royal Victorian Order in the Chapel of the Savoy are extremely beautiful and will delight all who examine them.

A coat of arms, complete with its accessories, is termed an Achievement, comprising the Shield, Crest, Helmet, Wreath, Mantling, Supporters and Motto (as shown in Fig 3). Of these, the Shield is the basic part, upon which are placed those devices

FIG. 4.

THE EFFIGY OF THE BLACK PRINCE IN
CANTERBURY CATHEDRAL (AFTER STOTHARD).

that in technical language are called charges, and these serve to give it its distinctive feature as applied to a particular individual or family. Next in importance is the Crest. A form of crest was used as a distinguishing mark for leaders in battle long before Heraldry was evolved, and it was not until some time after the science was established that the crest was incorporated as part of it.

The helmet appears in the composition, supporting the crest and is encircled by a wreath of twisted silk or cord. Six twists are usually illustrated.

Secured by the wreath and issuing from each side of the base of the crest is the mantling or lambrequin, originally used to protect the wearer from rain and sun. It is depicted now as being honourably torn in battle. Supporters, a more recent addition (fifteenth century) are to be seen on the Arms of Peers who are entitled to bear them by virtue of their rank. The number of commoners to whom the privilege of supporters has been accorded, is very limited.

The language of Heraldry to the uninitiated is a little confusing at first because it has been derived from the Norman French, although from long usage it has become Anglicized and is therefore pronounced as if it were English.

This, then, is the brief outline of the history and growth of Heraldry. The chief features of this science will be dealt with in detail in the succeeding chapters under their appropriate heading, and in addition the chapter at the end "See for Yourself" will enable the choicest examples to be easily found.

A short Bibliography is also provided for those who would make a wider study.

CHAPTER II

THE SHIELD OF ARMS

"Awake, awake, English nobility,
Let not sloth dim your honours new begot:
Cropp'd are the flower de luces in your arms;
Of England's coat one half is cut away."

(From Henry V's funeral scene, Henry VI, part I.)

SHAKESPEARE.

To describe a coat of arms correctly in Heraldic terms is to "BLAZON" it and with the SHIELD as the basis of all armorial bearings, since it was and still is the principal means of displaying an Heraldic device, it is essential in BLAZONING that the Shield should be quoted first of all. The surface of a shield is called the FIELD.

The earliest form used in connection with heraldic design was the Norman "KITE" Shield (Fig. 5A), with its long and tapering shape which was not really suitable for the display of arms.

To meet the military requirements of the age a smaller form was adopted in the thirteenth century and this was known as the HEATER shape (Fig. 5B) because of its resemblance to the base of a flat iron; this, too, in the fourteenth century was slightly modified (Fig. 5C) and is regarded even now as the finest of all the shapes for the display of Heraldry.

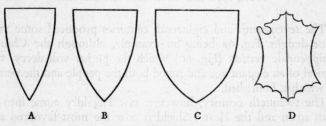

FIG. 5.

FOUR STAGES IN THE DEVELOPMENT OF THE SHIELD.

Later in the fourteenth century the design was changed again, this time the outline of the shield became more ornate, the surface and edges consisting of a series of concave curves (Fig. 5D). There are many examples of this shield to be seen wherever H.M. the Queen Mother's Arms are displayed. The reverse of a George VI half crown piece shows an example based on this type of shield.

In many instances a notch in the top left hand side was shown to support the lance, and when shown in this manner a shield was said to be à bouche.

With the introduction of classic forms into architecture in the late sixteenth and throughout the seventeenth century, the shape of the shield in many instances was varied to conform to the surrounding ornament. This form shown in Fig. 6A is to be found in St. Paul's Cathedral, the Colleges at Oxford, and on tombs and private houses up and down the country.

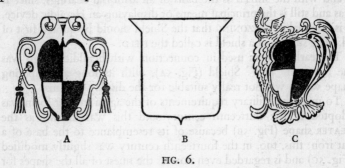

FIG. 6.

16TH, 17TH AND 18TH CENTURY DESIGNS.

The seventeenth and eighteenth centuries produced some very poor designs, Fig. 6B being an example, although the Chinese Chippendale version (Fig. 6C) which the purists will decry, was typical of an elegant age and suited both the people and the period in which it flourished.

The twentieth century, however, saw Heraldry come into its own again and the Heater Shield is now the most favoured and recommended shape for the display of arms.

To enable the charges on the FIELD to be blazoned correctly, the shield is divided up as indicated in Fig. 7. It is important to re-member that the DEXTER side of a shield is on the *left* of the viewer, and the SINISTER on the *right*. This rule also applies to supporters and any other devices displayed with the coat of arms, for example Fig. 3 shows the impaled achievement of the Fourth Marquis of Cholmondeley, namely, Cholmondeley impaling Kingscote.

Shakespeare emphasized the importance of the recognition of Coat Armour in Henry V's reign when at Agincourt he puts this phrase into the French Herald's mouth in his plea to Henry to:

> " . . . *wander o'er this bloody field*
> *To book our dead and then to bury them;*
> *To sort our nobles from our common men.*"

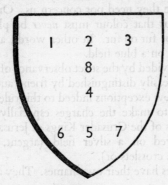

FIG. 7.

THE IMPORTANT POINTS ON A HERALDIC SHIELD.

1. DEXTER CHIEF POINT.	5. MIDDLE BASE.
2. MIDDLE CHIEF.	6. DEXTER BASE.
3. SINISTER CHIEF.	7. SINISTER BASE.
4. FESS POINT.	8. HONOUR POINT.

CHAPTER III

HERALDIC TINCTURES AND BLAZONING

THE coloured surfaces are called Tinctures and these can be of metal, colour, or fur, or a combination of two of these, as in a chequered coat. There are two metals, five colours and various forms of fur, out of which the following are most used:

Two metals – Gold and Silver
Five colours – Red, Blue, Green, Black and Purple
Two furs – Ermine and Vair

The remainder of the tinctures are rarely seen in English Heraldry so that at this stage they need not concern us. One of the golden rules of Heraldry is that colour must *never* be placed on colour, metal on metal, nor fur on fur. In other words, a red lion would never be displayed on a blue field.

The contrast provided by the strict observance of the rule enabled the warriors to be easily distinguished by friend and foe alike.

There are very few exceptions indeed to this rule, and these were deliberately done to make the charges especially exclusive. An instance is the arms of the Crusader Kings of Jerusalem where gold crosses are displayed on a silver field (argent, a cross potent between four plain crosslets or).

Heraldic tinctures have their own names. They are:

Gold – Or   Silver – Argent
Red – Gules   Blue – Azure
Green – Vert   Black – Sable
          Purple – Purpure

FIG. 8. HERALDIC TINCTURES — HATCHING.

The seventeenth century engravers introduced a system of dots and lines to indicate colours on their black and white illustrations termed HATCHING (Fig. 8). The older method of TRICKING by outline drawings with indications for colour here shown stippled for the reader's benefit (Figs. 9A and B) was far more satisfactory for

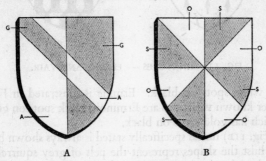

FIG. 9. TRICKING.

record purposes, but black and white illustrations nowadays are best shown in outline only, with SABLE indicated as solid black. By this means the quality in the drawing is unimpaired by dots and lines (Fig. 10).

In painting a coat of arms, gold can be represented by yellow, and silver by white, drawings on white paper being left blank to indicate silver. As to the density of colour used, this is left entirely to the artist's discretion, provided the colours are rich, for the glory of Heraldry is its wealth of colour, at no time perhaps more welcome than now.

Ermine has black spots on white, and Ermines (a variation of

FIG. 10.
ARMS OF OLIVER CROMWELL.

FIG. 11. TINCTURES — ERMINE AND VAIR.

Ermine) white spots on black. Ermine is illustrated in Fig. 11A. Two lesser known variations are Erminois, black spots on gold, and Pean which has gold spots on black.

Vair (Fig. 11B) unless specifically stated is always shown blue and white, whilst the shapes represent the pelt of grey squirrels. It is thought that these pelts were used for the lining of noblemen's cloaks and quite probably inspired this heraldic tincture. When vair is shown in any other colour it is termed VAIRY and the colour stated.

The alternatives to vair are shown in Fig. 12. They are POTENT and COUNTER POTENT and are of slightly different shape.

FIG. 12. TINCTURES — POTENT.

It must be borne in mind that heraldic language must always be very exact in its blazoning, omitting all unnecessary words yet retaining at the same time all the details in their correct order.

CHAPTER IV

PARTITION LINES

A SHIELD of Arms may consist entirely of a plain field of metal, colour, or fur, or a combination of two of the tinctures, by means of partition lines.

These dividing lines are illustrated in Fig. 13.

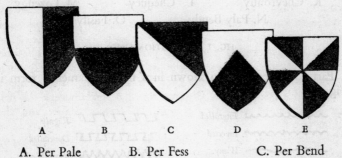

A. Per Pale   B. Per Fess   C. Per Bend

D. Per Chevron   E. Gyronny (of 8)

F. Quarterly or Per Cross   G. Per Saltire   H. Paly

I. Barry   J. Bendy

FIG. 13. PARTITION LINES.

21

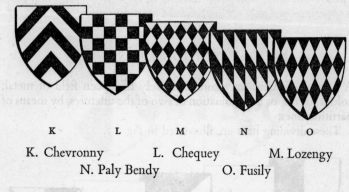

K　　　　　L　　　　　M　　　　　N　　　　　O

K. Chevronny　　　　L. Chequey　　　　M. Lozengy
N. Paly Bendy　　　　O. Fusily

FIG. 13. PARTITION LINES.

Partition lines are also shown in a more ornamental form in Fig. 14.

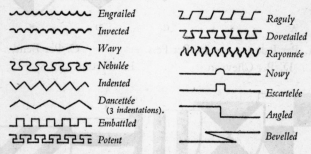

Engrailed		Raguly	
Invected		Dovetailed	
Wavy		Rayonnée	
Nebulée		Nowy	
Indented		Escartelée	
Dancettée (3 indentations).		Angled	
Embattled		Bevelled	
Potent			

FIG. 14. ORNAMENTAL PARTITION LINES.

Generally speaking there is no significance in their appearance on any particular shield and it is thought that they were evolved for the most part in the early days of Heraldry when design was simple and shields of arms fewer. The demand, however, in the succeeding centuries has brought about a certain amount of complication in design in an effort to maintain individuality. The rule of avoiding colour on colour, metal on metal, and fur on fur, applies equally to partitioned coats, but it is permissible to superimpose a charge on a "party" coloured field as for instance in Fig. 15A where a lion gules is superimposed on a chequered field or and azure.

A   B

FIG. 15. PARTY COLOURED AND COUNTERCHANGED COATS.

CHAPTER V

CHARGES

The Ordinaries and Sub-Ordinaries.

In an effort to vary still further the early heraldic design a new group of charges was created, some of which such as the Cross and Saltire, were no doubt inspired by the Church and Crusades. Other forms were probably accidental, taking their shape from the constructional segments and framework of the war shield itself.

The proportion of these charges in relation to the area of the field is illustrated in Fig. 16, but it is permissible to vary this slightly when used in conjunction with other charges.

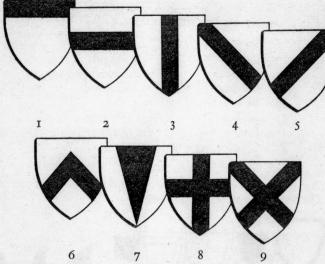

FIG. 16. CHARGES. THE ORDINARIES.

The Ordinaries, which are illustrated in Fig. 16, are:

1. The Chief	2. The Fess	3. The Pale
4. The Bend	5. The Bend Sinister	6. The Chevron
7. The Pile	8. The Cross	9. The Saltire

The Ordinaries may also (like the lines of partition) have their outer edges ornamentally treated by engrailing, etc.

It can safely be assumed that the cross as an heraldic charge owes its origin to the Crusades and has developed in many ways. Fox-Davies in his *Complete Guide to Heraldry* says that there are 400 varieties known to armoury or heraldic reference books, but it is doubtful whether more than thirty of these are in use, eighteen of which are quoted below. Here then are a few examples of which seven are illustrated (Fig. 17) in addition to the plain cross already illustrated:

9   10   11   12   14   15   18

FIG. 17. THE HERALDIC CROSS.

1.	Engrailed	2.	Embattled
3.	Indented	4.	Reguly
5.	Dovetailed	6.	Sacred or Passion
7.	Calvary	8.	Couped
9.	Botonny	10.	Flory
11.	Moline	12.	Potent
13.	Paté	14.	Patonce
15.	Crosslet	16.	Maltese
17.	Patriachal	18.	Crosslet-fitched

When quoting these they are all prefaced by the word CROSS. The Sub-Ordinaries (Fig. 18) are:

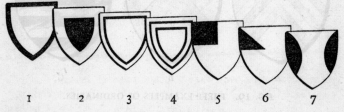

1   2   3   4   5   6   7

FIG. 18. THE SUB-ORDINARIES.

1. Bordure	2. Inescutcheon
3. Orle	4. Tressure
5. Canton	6. Gyron
7. Flanches	

8. Lozenge	9. Fusil
10. Mascle	11. Fret
12. Billet	13. Roundle
14. Label	

FIG. 18. THE SUB-ORDINARIES.

Fig. 19 illustrates three coats of arms which display ordinaries:

A. De Clare – – Or 3 Chevronnels gules
B. Fitzgerald – – Argent a Saltire gules
C. De Vallence – Barry argent and azure, over all an Orle of martlets gules.

FIG. 19. THREE EXAMPLES OF ORDINARIES.

CHAPTER VI

COMMON CHARGES

ANIMATE AND INANIMATE, PUNNING

*"They raged upon me with their mouths as
it were a ramping and roaring lion."*

Psalm 22, verse 13 from Guillim's
Display of Heraldry 1678 Edition.

THE lion heads the list as the most popular of all heraldic charges which includes animals, birds, fish, reptiles, flowers, trees, fruit and shells. To quote Boutell's *Heraldry* (revised by C. W. Scott-Giles, M.A.) *"anything which is capable of being depicted or symbolized in form or tincture may be a charge in Heraldry."*

Lions.

The rampant lion is the most imposing as well as the commonest of heraldic lions. He is to be found in various tinctures on inn signs all over the country. Lions have been borne by all the Sovereigns of England on their arms from the commencement of heraldry. Fig. 20 illustrates the various attitudes in which the heraldic lion may be displayed:

A.	Rampant	E.	Passant Guardant
B.	Passant	F.	Statant
C.	Sejant	G.	Couchant
D.	Sejant affronte (Scottish)		

(All facing dexter unless otherwise stated.)

The prefix "guardant" is used when the lion's head is turned to face the spectator as in the Royal Arms where the lions in the first and fourth quarters are "three lions passant guardant in pale, OR". Lions are normally portrayed with red tongues and claws (langued and armed) but if the lion or the field is gules, the tongues and claws must be coloured azure or a colour other than gules.

When three charges appear on a field it is assumed, unless other-

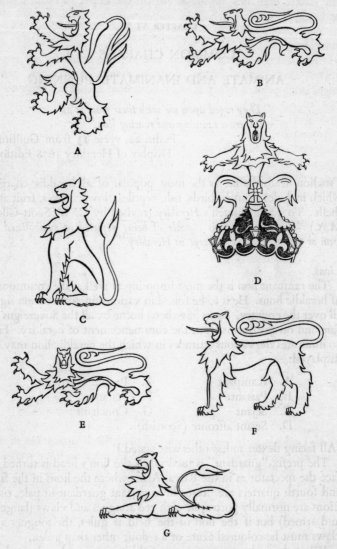

FIG. 20. THE HERALDIC LION.

wise stated, that they appear as two in the upper half and one in the base.

Other Animals.

Other animals having a certain amount of popularity are stags, wolves, bears, hares, horses, dogs, elephants, goats, cats, bulls, sheep, antelopes and squirrels. A walking stag is always "Trippant".

Birds.

Among the birds depicted in Heraldry, the eagle holds pride of place and is usually shown "Displayed" as in Fig. 22. A bird is termed "Close" when shown standing on the ground with folded wings. It is "Rising" when about to take wing, "Soaring" when flying upwards, and "Volant" when flying horizontally. When "Displayed" the head is usually shown turned to the dexter. When beaks and legs are of a different tincture from the rest of the bird they are said to be "beaked and membered" of whatever colour is

FIG. 21.   FIG. 22.   FIG. 23.

THE HERALDIC EAGLE.

used. Eagles may be shown crowned or collared as in some of the European royal arms, or they may bear a device on their wings as seen on the arms displayed outside many branches of Barclay's Bank (Fig. 21). No doubt the Heraldic eagle owes its origin to the Roman Eagle (Fig. 22). A thirteenth-century example may be seen in the wall arcading in the north aisle of Westminster Abbey (Fig. 23).

The swan and the pelican come next on the list. The swan

shown with a gold collar round its neck trailing a gold chain
(Fig. 24) "ducally gorged and chained", was used as a badge by
Henry V and can be seen on the Chantry over his tomb in Westminster Abbey. The pelican (Fig. 25) is usually associated with
the Church and is invariably depicted standing above its nest
wounding its breast in order to feed its young with its life blood.
The heraldic blazon is "a pelican in its piety". The Colleges of

| FIG. 24. | FIG. 25. | FIG. 26. |
| THE SWAN. | THE PELICAN. | THE BLACK PRINCE'S FEATHER. |

Corpus Christi at Oxford and Cambridge make use of this device
on their arms, and an excellent carved specimen is to be found over
the reredos in St. Mary Abchurch in the City of London.

The feathers of the ostrich are famous in English history as the
charge on the Black Prince's Shield of Peace and appear on his
tomb in Canterbury Cathedral (Fig. 26). The Martlet (heraldic

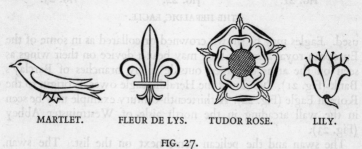

| MARTLET. | FLEUR DE LYS. | TUDOR ROSE. | LILY. |

FIG. 27.

swallow) which appears in the Arms of Westminster Abbey and School and University College, Oxford, are depicted minus feet (Fig. 27). It is to be assumed that the early artists portrayed devices only as they knew them and decided that as swallows were never to be found walking on the ground they were therefore without feet.

Fish.

The dolphin was the charge of the Dauphin of France who bore OR a dolphin azure quartered with the Arms of France. These arms were marshalled with her own arms by Mary Queen of Scots. Fish of all kinds have been borne as arms, particularly when the fish represents a surname. A fish is termed "Naiant" when swimming fesswise, "Uriant" when diving, and "Hauriant" when palewise with head to the top.

Shells.

The commonest "shell" charge is the escallop. It is also the emblem of St. James and is to be seen on the arms of the See of Rochester, Wadham College, and Merton College, Oxford. The whelk shell was used in the arms of the poet Shelley.

Reptiles and Insects.

The snake may be shown in three ways, knotted, coiled with head erect, or gliding. The grasshopper, the spider, and the bee are used also as devices. The former was the badge of Sir Thomas Gresham, founder of the Royal Exchange, and a giant grasshopper can be seen as a weather vane on the present Royal Exchange in London to commemorate this, whilst a modern coat of arms just inside the gateway to St. Bartholomew's Priory in the City of London shows a spider's web to commemorate Aston Webb the architect, and lastly a memorial outside St. Dunstan's in the West, Fleet Street, displays the bees in Lord Northcliffe's arms.

Monsters.

The following are the best known of the mythical beasts used as charges:

The Unicorn (to be found on the Royal Arms) (Fig. 69);

The Griffin   (one of the Marquess of Cholmondeley's supporters)
               (Fig. 3);
The Dragon   (the badge of the Principality of Wales;)
The Pegasus   (winged horse)—familiar nowadays as the badge
               of the famous Airborne Division which fought so
               gallantly at Arnhem. It is a comparatively rare
               charge, although it appears on the arms of the
               Inner Temple;
The Phœnix in flames (a badge of Queen Elizabeth) can also
               be seen over the south entrance to St. Paul's
               Cathedral and provides a very fitting emblem for
               Wren's masterpiece.

Trees and Plants.

Oaks as might be expected, are of course, very common in
English Heraldry. Other trees are also depicted, among them being
the apple, pear and chestnut, so too are the stumps of trees, branches,
sprigs and leaves. A tree is usually shown "proper" (natural
colouring) and if uprooted is termed "eradicated". A fruit tree is
termed "fructed", whilst an oak tree is "acorned". Colonel Carlos
was granted arms incorporating an oak tree and royal crowns for
the part he played in Charles II's escape at Boscobel. Beckenham in
the County of Kent has a modern coat incorporating chestnut trees
which is an allusion to the chestnut tree-lined roads in the borough
(Fig. 72).

The sprig of the broom plant (Planta genista) is famous as the
badge of the Plantagenets and is pounced on the brass effigy of
Richard II in Westminster Abbey. It appears also in the modern
grant of arms of Bromley, Kent.

Wheatsheafs (garbs) are to be found on the arms of the Marquess
of Cholmondeley (Fig. 3) and in the arms of the Earls of Chester.

The fleur de lys (Fig. 27B) and the Tudor rose (Fig. 27C) are
the two most common floral designs.

There are a number of versions of the fleur de lys, but particularly fine examples can be seen on the handsome doors to
Henry VII's Chapel and on his tomb in Westminster Abbey. The
Black Prince's effigy in Canterbury Cathedral displays some beautiful specimens too. (Fig. 4).

The fleurs de lys were removed from the Royal Arms in 1801, but they still appear in the Scottish quarter as part of the tressure surrounding the rampant lion. The "Tudor" rose is the dog rose and with the marriage of Henry VII (Lancaster) to Elizabeth of York, the red and white roses were united and blazoned a rose argent charged upon a rose gules, slipped and leaved proper (Fig. 27c), which means that the seeds in the centre are gold and the sepals green. The lily is found on the arms of Eton College and Magdalen College, Oxford (Fig. 27d).

Celestial Bodies.

The sun with its surrounding rays is termed "in its splendour". The sun in its splendour was the badge of Edward IV and Shakespeare refers to it in his tragedy of King Richard III when Gloucester opens the play with these words:

"*Now is the winter of discontent made glorious summer by this sun of York.*"

Stars are termed Estoiles and have wavy rays. They must not be confused with the Mullet which has straight rays and is sometimes pierced.

Inanimate Objects.

The list of charges under this heading is immense and some of the more popular objects only are quoted here, namely:

Battle axe, armour, bell, book, buckle, bow, hunting horn, castle, chessrook, crescent, cross, crown, crozier, lymphad (galley), glove, globe, harp, helmet, horseshoe, maunche (sleeve)

FIG. 28. THE MAUNCHE.

(Fig. 28), millrind, pheon (arrowhead), portcullis, sword, spur, torch, beacon, water bouget, wheel.

The City of Sheffield has a sheaf of arrows in its arms, whilst the Bowes family (H.M. the Queen Mother) use three bows palewise on an ermine field. A glove between two estoiles is depicted on the arms of Capt. Cook, 1728–79. A maunche gules on a field or, was the arms of Warren Hastings, 1732–1818. The harp is the well-known device in the "Irish" quarter of the English Royal Arms (Fig. 29). William Morris bore horseshoes on his arms. The

FIG. 29. THE HARP.

portcullis (Fig. 30), the badge of the Beaufort family, can be seen in Henry VII's Chapel, and on the arms of Westminster Abbey School and in the arms of Westminster City too. The pheon is portrayed in the arms of Philip Sidney, whose family resided at Penshurst (Fig. 31). A modern inn sign in this village also displays

FIG. 30. THE PORTCULLIS.   FIG. 31. THE PHEON.

the azure pheon. The water bouget is illustrated in Fig. 32 and was used by the Roos and Bouchier families and can be seen in the ruins of Kirkham Abbey, the Cloisters of Canterbury Cathedral, and in the arms of Ilfracombe.

FIG. 32. THE WATER BOUGET.

Canting Arms.

In the early days of Heraldry, surnames in many cases lent themselves to some form of illustration and thus began canting or punning arms all over the country.

A few examples picked at random will serve to illustrate this point; the charges follow the surnames and are bracketed for quick reference.

Arches	(Arches)
Dauphin	(Dolphin)
Glasscock	(Cockerels)
Rookwood	(Chessrooks)
Corbet	(Ravens—Corbies)
Farrer	(Horseshoes)
Lucy	(Lucies—pike)
Shelley	(Shells)
Trumpington	(Trumpets)
Wingate	(Portcullis)
Shakespeare	(Shaking spear or tilting lance)
Webb	(Spider's web)

The custom is still continued and the modern coat of Sir Aston Webb, who gave Buckingham Palace its modern exterior, at St. Bartholomew's Church, London, mentioned earlier in this chapter, is an example.

CHAPTER VII

CRESTS, HELMETS, WREATHS, MANTLING, SUPPORTERS AND MOTTOES

"Now by my father's badge, old Nevil's crest,
The rampant bear chain'd to the ragged staff,
This day I'll wear aloft my burgonet."

King Henry VI, Part II.

The Crest.

Long before Heraldry came into being a form of crest was used to surmount a helmet as a means of decoration and to ward off any downward blow aimed at the wearer's head.

Early English manuscripts show the heraldic crest fan shaped with the device painted on the side; then followed the carved crest of wood, but used mainly on funeral helms and another type of boiled leather and canvas covered with stamped gesso; the crest on the funeral helm over the Black Prince's tomb in Canterbury Cathedral was made in this way. Two very fine series of crests surmount the Stalls of the Knights of the Garter at St. George's Chapel, Windsor, and the Knights of the Bath in Henry VII's Chapel, Westminster Abbey, and our Cathedrals and many of our Parish Churches possess specimens on monumental effigies and brasses.

To quote but a few, the effigy of the Black Prince, the finest of its kind in the world (1376) rests on a helmet with a crowned lion for a crest (Fig. 4). The griffin's head appears under the head of Sir John de Montacute (1389) in Salisbury Cathedral; a calf's head surmounts the helmet of Sir Hugh Calverley, companion to the Black Prince on his fine monument (1393) at Bunbury, Cheshire, whilst the effigy in Wingfield Church, Suffolk, of John de la Pole, Duke of Suffolk (1491) shows his head resting on a helm with a savage's head for a crest.

Two noteworthy modern Royal crests can be seen on the reverse side of the English and Scottish one shilling pieces.

So many people erroneously refer to the coat of arms of a family, or school, as a family crest or school crest, that it cannot be too strongly emphasized that *the crest is the device which surmounts the helmet only*, and must not be confused with a coat of arms of which it is only part.

It is quite possible that the fashion of having crests engraved on family plate for some 200 years has been responsible for this misnomer.

Occasionally, one can see a crest on the door panel of a limousine, but this custom is on the wane.

The Helmet.

From its inception until the seventeenth century only one type of helmet was used in heraldic display as we can see for ourselves on the early stall plates at Windsor (1421). During the Stuart period the shape and position was varied to indicate rank, although the designs up to the start of the twentieth century were poor indeed, for it would have been almost impossible for any man to have worn these ornamental "footballs". The present version is nearer the traditional tournament helmet and that of the Esquire bears a strong resemblance to the famous BROCAS helm in the Tower of London Armouries.

Fig. 33 illustrates from left to right the modern version of the helmet of the Esquire, B being an alternative to A, Knight and

FIG. 33. HERALDIC HELMETS.

Baronet, Peer and Sovereign, that of an Esquire is of steel with a closed visor, that of a Knight steel with an open visor. The helmet of a Peer is of silver with gold grills whilst that of the Sovereign is of gold, full face (affronte) with grills guarding the facial opening. A helmet shown in profile faces dexter, a suitable height should be three quarters the length of the shield. It is a common error to portray the helmet too small in proportion to its shield.

The Wreath.

The base of the crest is surrounded by a wreath of twisted silk, usually of six twists of the two main tinctures of the arms. The wreath resembles the head-band of an Arab Chief's headdress and quite probably both originate from the same source.

The seventeenth, eighteenth and nineteenth century illustrations often depicted the wreath as a straight bar seesawing on the top of the helmet, whereas it should encircle the top of the helmet (Fig. 3).

Mantling.

The mantling or lambrequin is the elegant flowing drapery which at first served a useful purpose in protecting the wearer from the rays of the tropical sun in much the same way as does the head-dress of the French Foreign Legionnaire to-day.

In the heat of battle its edges became jagged, a feature represented by the scalloped edges, although this is not essential, and it is left to the discretion of the artist providing the rules regarding tinctures are observed.

Mantling is shown of two tinctures and the technical description is "doubled". In other words, red lined with silver would be termed "Gules doubled argent".

Supporters.

Supporters are the creatures both real and mythical balanced on either side of the shield. Their duty is to support the shield and because of their imposing appearance supporters as well as crests were excellent subjects for display on the gate piers at the entrances to many of England's stately homes. A century ago some amusing versions appeared, chiefly over the old shop-fronts whose owners were privileged to supply the Royal Household, where supporters were depicted reclining gracefully on each side of the shield. One still exists in Jermyn Street, Piccadilly, London, and no doubt many more abound in London, Windsor and Edinburgh. The Bull Hotel at Rochester and the Rose and Crown Hotel at Tonbridge, Kent, have reclining supporters over the entrances. Two newspapers, *The Times* (Fig. 34) and the *Sunday Times* retain this form of Royal Arms in the headings of their front page, and even Buckingham Palace is so adorned at the south end of the main front!

THE TIMES

FIG. 34. THE ROYAL ARMS FROM "THE TIMES".

Some very fine specimens can be seen on the moat bridge at Hampton Court designed by Rev. E. E. Dorling, M.A., and at St. Stephen's entrance to the House of Commons designed by Pugin, the great Victorian "imbued with the medieval spirit" as G. W. Eve refers to him in *Heraldry as Art*. Eve himself was the greatest heraldic artist at the start of the century.

The seals still attached to historical documents in the Public Record Office and in our museums can show a great variety of supporters, for it was on the seals that they first appeared.

They may be borne only on the arms of Peers of the Realm, Knights of the three Orders, the Garter, Thistle, and St. Patrick, and Knights Grand Cross of other Orders. The supporters of Peers are hereditary whilst those of Knights Grand Cross are not.

The ornamental scroll or as it was termed "gas bracket" until recently considered correct, is now superseded by the mount vert (or green mound) as a base on which the shield and supporters now stand Figs. 66, 69 and 76.

The Motto.

A motto in England can be assumed and is not part of the official grant of arms. It can be in any language and owes its origin to war cries of the followers of feudal lords.

Henry V before Harfleur (Act 3, Scene I) ends his exhortation with . . . "Cry God for Harry! England and St. George". No doubt many of the war cries of the feudal ages were as spontaneous as the shouts of encouragement at a football match to-day, although a battle cry was usually a short sentence based often on the device on the arms or crest of a war leader.

In Scotland the motto is registered, and Sir Thomas Innes of Learney in his very excellent book on Scottish Heraldry states that the matriculation specifies whether the position of the motto is above the crest or below the shield, the latter position being assigned only when two mottoes are registered.

CHAPTER VIII

CROWNS, CORONETS AND MITRES

THE war helms of Kings and Princes were adorned with crowns that they might be easily recognized on the field of battle by friend and foe alike. A simple form of coronet not only adorns the helm of the Black Prince's effigy, but the lion on his crested helmet is similarly crowned.

Various examples of the Royal Crown are borne on the Great Seals of England exhibited in the British Museum where it will be seen that the Crown has undergone several changes since Edward the Confessor's time, although the present type was used first in Henry V's reign. A carved scene over his Chantry in Westminster Abbey depicts his coronation with this form of crown.

A prolific display of crowns can be seen in the wall spaces between the great windows inside King's College Chapel, Cambridge (Henry VI) whilst the great candleholders on the tomb of Henry VII in Westminster Abbey show crowns without arches resting on a Tudor rose.

The heraldic crown as we knew it (Fig. 35) until Her Majesty the Queen adopted the bowed arched crown (frontispiece) had not been changed since the latter part of Queen Victoria's reign, and we are no doubt familiar with its appearance on Royal Mail vans, whilst the present one shilling and two shilling pieces have excellent modern crowns on their reverse sides.

In addition to the English Royal Crown, there are many coronets in use not only in Heraldry but at every coronation ceremony when they are worn by children of the Sovereign and by Dukes, Marquesses, Earls, Viscounts and Barons. The Kings of Arms wear crowns as befits their rank.

The coronet of the Prince of Wales (Fig. 36(A)) is like the Royal Crown but with one intersecting arch instead of two. The younger children of the Sovereign have coronets (B) of the same pattern minus the arches.

The heraldic version of the coronet of a Duke (C) carries five gold and a barry wavy that of a Marquess (o) also with three gold . . . . two silver balls. An Earl . . . . on his coronet has five . . . . on points with . . . . betw . . . . Viscount's (1) . . . . Bar . . . . four silver balls . . . . round the rim . . . . .

The . . . . three Kings . . . . two piles with . . . . you.

Three p . . . . ualitions are the . . . . . . al and Aug. Leo c . . . . it appears mainly on . . . . A uniform varie . . . . and (fig. 174).

FIG. 35.   FIG. 36A.

THE ROYAL CROWN — TWO EXAMPLES.

FIG. 36B.   FIG. 36C.   FIG. 36D.

FIG. 36E.   FIG. 36F.   FIG. 36G.

rank . . . . It can be sw . . . . of one of the three figures . . . . a Viscount in the C . . . . ondon. The . . . . the Naval . . . . . (fig. 170) was awarded to distinguished sailors and is borne on the arms of Lord Nelson. Lastly, the air . . . crown, a newcomer (fig. 172) is similarly awarded to . . . . Royal Air Force . . . . . .

Crowns are emblematic . . . . H.B., Colchester and Bury St. Edmund, the . . . . ex and East Anglia, and the University of Oxf . . . .

The Royal Crown . . . . it as a basis for the arms of the Douglas family . . . . the Duke of Hamilton and Marshal of the Royal Air Force Sir William Sholto Douglas. The historian F . . . . quotes the

FIG. 36H.

FIG. 36. CROWNS AND CORONETS.

gold strawberry leaves, that of a Marquess (D) alternately three gold strawberry leaves and two silver balls. An Earl (E) on his coronet has five silver balls raised on points with gold strawberry leaves between the points. A Viscount's (F) has nine silver balls, whilst a Baron (G) has a coronet of four silver balls at equal distances round the rim.

The crowns worn by the three Kings of Arms are of silver gilt with nine oak leaves as in Fig. 36H.

Three purely heraldic additions are the Mural, Naval and Air Force crowns. The first appears mainly on civic arms. A curious variety surmounts the arms of the London County Council (Fig. 37A)

A   B   C

FIG. 37. MURAL, NAVAL AND ASTRAL CROWNS.

and it was also at one time granted sparingly to soldiers of fame. It can be seen on the head of one of the bronze figures on Holborn Viaduct in the City of London. The second, the Naval crown (Fig. 37B) was awarded to distinguished sailors and is borne on the arms of Lord Nelson. Lastly, the astral crown, a newcomer (Fig. 37C) is similarly awarded to members of the Royal Air Force.

Crowns are emblazoned on the arms of Hull, Colchester and Bury St. Edmunds, the counties of Middlesex and East Anglia, and the University of Oxford.

The Royal Crown surmounting a red heart is borne on the arms of the Douglas family (His Grace the Duke of Hamilton and Marshal of the Royal Air Force Sir William Sholto-Douglas). The historian Froissart (1338–1410) in his chronicles quotes the incident which is perpetuated in these arms by telling us that Sir James Douglas was enlisted by King Robert with the task of conveying his embalmed heart, after his death, to the Holy Sepulchre at Jerusalem. *"Let it be known ye carry with you the heart of King Robert of Scotland at his instance and desire to be presented to the Holy Sepulchre."* The King died on 7th November, 1337 and was buried in the Abbey of Dunfermline. Douglas became involved during his mission in a fight between the Kings of Spain and Granada, when on finding himself surrounded he hurled the heart forward and then perished in the fight.

Scottish Airlines with whom the Duke of Hamilton has connections bear this famous charge on their 'planes and on the cap badges of the aircraft officers (Fig. 80).

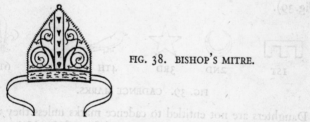

FIG. 38. BISHOP'S MITRE.

The arms of Archbishops and Bishops are surmounted by a mitre (Fig. 38) instead of a helmet. The Bishopric of Durham however was until the beginning of the last century a Palatinate (the province of one enjoying Royal privileges). This is commemorated in the arms. In place of the two crosiers usually shown is a sword and crozier in saltire, whilst the mitre which surmounts the arms is placed within a ducal coronet.

CHAPTER IX

CADENCE MARKS, DIFFERENCING,
BADGES AND KNOTS

CADENCE marks or Differences are distinguishing marks applied to
coats of arms to indicate various branches and cadets of a family.

There are cadence marks for the first nine sons!—six of which
are illustrated. The label indicating the first son is borne only
during his father's lifetime, whilst those for the younger sons are
permanent and are generally borne on the chief unless the shield is
quartered, when they are borne on the centre or fess-point
(Fig. 39).

1ST   2ND   3RD   4TH   5TH   6TH

FIG. 39. CADENCE MARKS.

Daughters are not entitled to cadence marks unless they are the
children of the Sovereign. The personal flag of Her Majesty when
Princess Elizabeth and which flew over Clarence House when Her
Royal Highness was in residence, bore a label of three points. In
England, sons may bear the arms of their father with the appropriate cadence mark, but in Scotland it is customary for them to
petition the Lord Lyon King of Arms for a "matriculation" of their
paternal arms, in other words they ask that their father's arms may
be suitably differenced to indicate their position within their family,
and until this is granted they may not assume arms. The difference
is usually a form of bordure.

Once again the effigy of the Black Prince in Canterbury Cathedral
provides us with an example of a label as the mark of the first son
(Fig. 4). He bears a label of three points on his surcoat, although
strangely enough the shield hanging over his tomb is without one.

In the south aisle of the nave of Westminster Abbey there is a
thirteenth-century shield representing the arms of Henry de Lacy,

Earl of Lincoln, quarterly or and gules, a baston sable, a label of five points argent. Modern labels are usually of three points only as will be seen in Fig. 39 although the shield of the Duke of Kent (grandson of George V) bears a label of five points.

Prior to the fifteenth century when cadence marks were standardized, shields were differenced either by changing the tincture or the charges, or by the addition as in Scotland of the bordure. The existing charges were sometimes varied, but in every case the principal feature was retained.

An example of the bordure can be seen in Southwark Cathedral where on a pillar in the south aisle is carved the shield (fifteenth century) and Cardinal's hat of Cardinal Beaufort son of "old John of Gaunt, time-honoured Lancaster". The colours in recent years have been restored and show the arms of France and England quartered within a bordure compony (alternate argent and azure squares) the colours of the Lancastrians.

There is no such charge in heraldry as a Bar Sinister. The term is BEND Sinister and it does not necessarily denote bastardy, although an abbreviated version, the BATON Sinister, was certainly borne by the illegitimate sons of Edward IV, Henry VIII, Charles II, James II and William IV.

Badges.

The Yeomen Warders of the Tower of London wear a device on their tunics depicting the floral emblems of the three kingdoms, England, Scotland and Ireland. The rose in the centre has a thistle on one side and the shamrock on the other, the whole device being surmounted by the crown. This then is a badge, and like all badges is no official part of an achievement of arms, neither is a badge hereditary. Regimental badges and divisional signs are the successors to the medieval badges which identified the members of the household of a feudal lord, just as the badge of the Yeomen Warders indicates their service to Her Majesty.

The Battle of Britain window which replaces the easternmost window of Henry VII's chapel, Westminster Abbey, destroyed in the blitz, contains the heraldic badges of sixty-three Fighter Squadrons of the Royal Air Force which took part in the Battle of Britain. The blaze of colour produced by this wonderful collection of badges is remarkable. The window is one of several designed by Mr. Hugh Easton for the Abbey and was dedicated in the presence of his late Majesty King George VI on the 10th July, 1947. The style used by Mr. Easton very much resembles that designed by Pugin for the glass in the Royal Gallery of the Houses of Parliament and illustrated in G. W. Eve's book *Heraldry as Art* (1907).

The cross of St. George, encircled by the garter, is the badge of the Order of the Garter and is worn on the robes of the Knights of that illustrious Order (Fig. 40).

FIG. 40. BADGE OF THE
ORDER OF THE GARTER.

In addition to household badges there are the personal badges of which the crown encircled ostrich feathers of the heir apparent to the throne is an excellent example (Fig. 41).

FIG. 41. BADGE OF THE
PRINCE OF WALES.

"*The red rose and the white are on his face,
The fatal colours of our striving houses.*"
SHAKESPEARE, Henry VI, Part III.

Two famous badges are the red and the white roses, emblems of the Wars of the Roses said to have been plucked by the leaders of the opposing sides in the Temple Gardens, London, the White Rose for York and the Red Rose for Lancaster. After the marriage of Henry VII to Elizabeth of York the roses were combined to symbolize the amalgamation of the two rival houses, as can be seen in King's College, Cambridge.

The Broom Plant (Planta genista) and the White Hart were badges of Richard II, and over the entrance to the White Hart Hotel in Bromley, Kent, is a very fine specimen of this Royal emblem, whilst in the same town the planta genista badge adorns the keystone on the new municipal buildings. The White Hart is to be found also on the effigy of Richard II in Westminster Abbey (Fig. 42), and as a mural in the Abbey Muniment Room.

The Bear and Ragged Staff, the well-known badge of the Earl of Warwick, is much in evidence in the old town of that name. The Falcon and Fetterlock (Fig. 43) and the Portcullis were the badges of Henry VII and form part of the pattern on the beautiful bronze gates to his chapel.

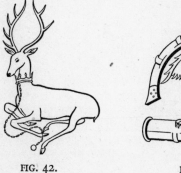

FIG. 42. FIG. 43.

THE WHITE HART. THE FALCON AND FETTERLOCK.

Knots.

Heraldic knots look very much like the illustrations one sees on Boy Scouts' knot tying diagrams. They are a small class indeed among heraldic devices and perhaps the best known of them all is

FIG. 44. THE STAFFORD KNOT.

the Stafford Knot (Fig. 44) which can often be found on industrial pottery made in Staffordshire. Two others are the Bourchier and the Heneage Knots (Figs. 45 and 46).

FIG. 45.

THE BOURCHIER KNOT.

FIG. 46.

THE HENEAGE KNOT.

CHAPTER X

MARSHALLING OF ARMS

THE grouping of arms for the purpose of indicating Sovereignty, Office, alliance or descent, is termed "marshalling".

The grouping of arms into one composition is effected in three ways, dimidiation, impalement and quartering. The first method and the oldest form of marshalling is illustrated in Fig. 47, the dexter half of the husband's coat being placed on one side and the sinister half of the wife's on the other. This method was short-lived, for to cut a charge in half as dimidiation did, particularly where "ordinaries" were the charges, was most unsatisfactory.

FIG. 47.

DIMIDIATED ARMS

The next stage of development was impalement whereby the arms of the husband were placed side by side, and without alteration, with those of his wife within the area of the shield (Fig. 48A). This method is used to-day.

When the husband has been invested with a Knightly Order he is entitled to encircle his arms with the collar of that Order, or the Garter if it be the Order of the Garter, but he cannot impale the arms of his wife on this particular shield. It is necessary therefore in this instance to portray two shields, the second shield bearing the arms of his wife impaled with those of her husband and surrounded by a laurel wreath to balance the design.

The exceptions to this ruling are the arms of Her Majesty the

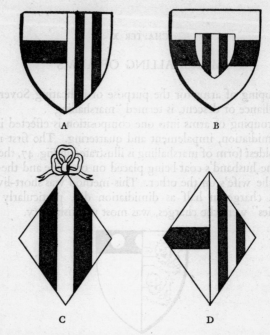

FIG. 48. THE MARSHALLING OF ARMS.

Queen, Queen Elizabeth the Queen Mother, and Queen Mary, who are ladies of the Most Noble Order of the Garter and therefore encircle their arms with the Garter by virtue of this. Two examples of these arms can be seen in the new heraldic stained glass windows in the partly rebuilt blitzed church of All Hallows by the Tower. Two shields in the east window illustrate the arms of Queen Elizabeth the Queen Mother as the Queen and as Duchess of York. In both instances the shields are surrounded with the Garter. A further very recent example can be seen in the ceiling of one of the oriel windows of the magnificent Hall of the Middle Temple portraying the arms of the Queen Mother with supporters.

Archbishops and bishops impale the arms of their See with their own personal arms on the sinister. The shield is surmounted by a mitre and two croziers are sometimes placed in saltire behind the shield.

The three Kings of Arms likewise impale their own personal arms with those of their office.

A man who marries an heiress is entitled to bear his wife's paternal arms in pretence. (Fig. 48B.)

Since divorce nullifies marriage, the arms of those concerned should revert to their bachelor and spinster states.

The children of an heiress only are permitted to quarter the arms of their parents, 1 and 4 representing the arms of their father, 2 and 3 those of their mother. This method of numbering quarterings from left to right, row by row, holds good for any number of quarterings, the paternal coat always being the first quarter and if the quarterings are of uneven number the paternal coat is then repeated in the last quarter.

The intermarriage between members of armigerous families has naturally added to the number of quarterings which their descendants can display. Fox-Davies in his very fine work *Armorial Families*, quotes for example the arms of Lloyd of Stockton in Chirbury, Shropshire, displaying 356 quarterings. The use of all these quarterings is, of course, optional.

An unmarried lady may bear her paternal arms on a lozenge (Fig. 48C), often surmounted by a lover's knot; on marrying she impales these arms with those of her husband and on becoming a widow she reverts to the lozenge but with her arms still impaled with those of her husband (Fig. 48D). Illustrations of the lozenge can be found on tombs and memorials throughout the country. There is an excellent example in Westminster Abbey on the monument to Frances Brandon, Duchess of Suffolk, Ob. 1559; another on the hearse monument to the Countess of Derby, Ob. 1636 in Harefield Church, Middlesex, and among the very handsome tombs at Framlingham, Suffolk, to the Fitzroys and the Howards of Henry VIII's reign.

CHAPTER XI

HATCHMENTS

THE word Hatchment is derived from "Achievement". A hatchment is simply an escutcheon of mourning painted on canvas or wood, about 4 ft. 6 in. square, and always displayed lozengewise. At the death of the person whose arms are borne thereon it is usually hung over the main entrance of the house during the period of mourning, and afterwards is displayed within the church of interment.

The custom of displaying hatchments started in the latter part of the seventeenth century, no doubt encouraged by the restoration of the monarchy, and almost vanishing as an art towards the end of the last century. Although the recently revised edition of Boutell's *Heraldry* states that the custom is not now observed, this is hardly correct, for the author has himself been responsible for the painting of three during the last four years, one in 1948 and two in 1951. This is also borne out by the correspondence to the Editor of the *Sunday Times* about three years ago and also within the last few months:

"I well remember seeing a hatchment fixed over the front door of the Earl of Powis's house on the west side of Berkeley Square after the death of the 3rd Earl in 1891. The hatchment was in position for some weeks."

"I saw one outside the gates of Donhead House, Shaftesbury, in about 1920 after the death of Sir James Pender."

"As recently as 1925 we were spending the summer at a house in Eaton Square when a very old lady died in a house opposite. The hatchment was hung over the front door."

"On the death of the Rector of Exeter College, Oxford (Dr. R. R. Marrett) in 1944 a hatchment was hung over the main gate of the College."

"I have the clearest recollection of having seen a hatchment hanging over the front door of the lodge at Eton less than 12

months ago after the death of Sir Henry Marten, the Provost.
A similar hatchment was hung in the same position and place in
1936 when Provost 'Monty' James died."

"Recently I went to the funeral of my old friend the Squire
of Nazeing and head of the family of Palmer. When I went to
the house I saw over the front door a hatchment bearing the
family's coat of arms."

Readers of *Vanity Fair* will probably remember the hatchment
seen by that dominating personality Becky Sharp on her first visit
to Sir Pitt Crawley, and again those she saw some years later over
the entrance at Queens Crawley.

There are, of course, many hatchments still hanging in our
cathedrals and churches, usually in that part used as a private chapel.
During the drastic restorations in the last century many were trans-
ferred to the end of the church and where possible to the base of the
bell tower.

The interest in hatchments is not merely in the grant of arms displayed, but in the treatment of the background also.

The background is all black on the hatchment of a bachelor

CASSIS VIRTUS

TUTISSIMA

FIG. 49. HATCHMENT
OF A MARRIED MAN.

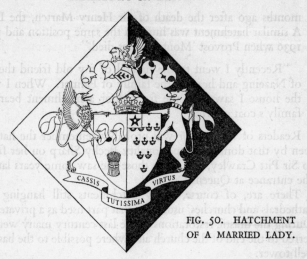

FIG. 50. HATCHMENT
OF A MARRIED LADY.

whilst the dexter half only is black when the deceased, a married
man, is survived by his wife (Fig. 49). The sinister half is black
when a married lady predeceases her husband (Fig. 50) and when a
widower dies the whole of the background is black (Fig. 51).

FIG. 51. COMBINED
HATCHMENT OF MARRIED
MAN AND HIS WIFE.

A spinster's arms are, of course, displayed within a lozenge on the hatchment surmounted by a lover's knot, surrounded by a black background as are those of a widow, but in this instance the arms are shown impaled with those of her husband.

The hatchment illustrated on the cover of this book was commissioned in 1951 by the (present) 5th Marquess of Cholmondeley, Hereditary Lord Great Chamberlain of England to our new Sovereign Queen Elizabeth II. Contrary to custom this hatchment was painted nearly thirty years after the death of the 4th Marquess (1858–1923) whose wife Ida (daughter of Col. Sir Robert Nigel Fitzhardinge Kingscote, K.C.B.) died in 1938. This hatchment, which hangs in the private chapel at Cholmondeley Castle, Malpas, Cheshire, completes a very fine series of hatchments which hang there and at Houghton Hall, Norfolk.

It is assumed that most hatchments were painted during the lifetime of those whose memory they perpetuate, and that the background was painted in after death. They are for the most part the work of local artists and vary in quality considerably.

The arms of the three Kings of Arms, bishops, deans and heads of colleges, may be impaled with their official arms on hatchments; their official arms on the dexter side and their personal arms on the sinister, whilst the background must be black only behind their personal arms.

A hatchment seen in Oxford only a few months ago bearing the arms of the late Warden, Mr. B. H. Summers, impaled by those of All Souls College, caused some comment from heraldry enthusiasts because the whole of the background had been painted black, thereby announcing the decease of the college as well.

The funeral railway coach used to convey the body of his late Majesty King George VI is painted with a hatchment displaying the Royal Arms within the Garter surmounted by a crown. A very rare example indeed of a Royal funeral hatchment.

The parish church of Chiddingstone in the Weald of Kent, possesses thirteen hatchments commemorating members of the Streatfeild family and date from 1645 to 1852.

CHAPTER XII

ORDERS OF KNIGHTHOOD

"As touching the qualifications which formerly made persons capable of this honour of Knighthood, the principal and remarkable were these three, Merit, Birth, and Estate."

Ashmole's "Order of the Garter".

1. THE MOST NOBLE ORDER OF THE GARTER.

The Most Noble Order of the Garter takes precedence over the eight Orders dealt with in this chapter. Elias Ashmole in his celebrated work *The Institution of the Most Noble Order of the Garter* published in 1672 says the Order was founded by Edward III in the 23rd year of his reign (1350), and that "it exceeds in Majesty, Honour and Fame all chivalrous Orders in the world". He suggests that the circular garter badge of the Order owes its origin to the round table set up in Windsor Castle by Edward III for the feasts held there during the jousting between the Knights of Christendom. Fig. 52 shows the star embodying the cross of St. George encircled by the Garter. The Order comprises twenty-five Knights Companions in addition to the Sovereign, sons of the Sovereign and foreign monarchs. Knights of the Garter may encircle their shields with the Garter, a custom started during Henry VIII's reign. The Chapel of the Order is St. George's Chapel, Windsor Castle, where the banners, crests and stall plates may be seen (See also Chapter XVI).

The twenty-five Founder Companions were:

> Edward Plantagenet (The Black Prince)
> Henry Plantagenet, Duke of Lancaster
> Thomas de Beauchamp, Earl of Warwick
> John de Grailly, Captal de Buch
> Ralph de Stafford, Earl of Stafford
> William de Montacute, Earl of Salisbury
> Roger de Mortimer, Earl of March
> John de Lisle, Lord Lisle of Rougemont
> Bartholomew Burghersh, Lord Burghersh

FIG. 52. STAR OF THE ORDER OF THE GARTER.

John de Beauchamp, Lord Beauchamp de Warwick
John de Mohun, Lord Mohun of Dunster
Sir Hugh Courtenay
Thomas Holland, Earl of Kent
John de Grey, Lord Grey of Rotherfield
Sir Richard Fitz-Simon
Sir Miles Stapleton
Sir Thomas Wale
Sir Hugh Wrottesley
Sir Nele Loryng
Sir John Chandos
Sir James Audley
Sir Otto Holland
Sir Henry D'Enne
Sir Sanchet D'Alrichecourt
Sir Walter Paveley

"When first this Order was ordained, my Lords,
Knights of the Garter were of noble birth,
Valiant and virtuous, full of haughty courage,
Such as were grown to credit by the wars;
Not fearing death, nor shrinking for distress,
But always resolute in most extremes.
He that is not furnished in this sort
Doth but usurp the Sacred name of Knight
Profaning this most Honourable Order."

Shakespeare, *Henry VI*, Part I, Act IV, Scene I.

2. THE MOST ANCIENT AND MOST NOBLE ORDER OF THE THISTLE.

The origin of this Order is lost in antiquity although it is known for certain that it was restored in 1540, and revived again in 1687 by James II. By a statute passed on the coronation of George IV the Order consists of the Sovereign and sixteen Knights. The badge of the Order pendant from the collar is a figure of St. Andrew bearing before him a white saltire (Fig. 53). During the religious disturbances in the reign of James, the Chapel of the Order was wrecked by the angry townsfolk of Edinburgh. The Order was

FIG. 53. BADGE OF THE
ORDER OF THE THISTLE.

not restored again until revived by Queen Anne when six more noblemen were added to it. The Order, which is one of the most exclusive, has never admitted a foreigner, and only one commoner.

The new Thistle Chapel in St. Giles' Cathedral, Edinburgh, was dedicated in the presence of King George V in 1911. In the roof are to be seen the shields of fourteen of the original knights, whilst the panelling at the backs of the stalls bears the modern stall plates of the Knights of the Order (See also Chapter XVI).

The Lord Lyon is King of Arms of the Most Ancient and Most Noble Order of the Thistle.

3. THE MOST ILLUSTRIOUS ORDER OF ST. PATRICK.

This Order, instituted by George III on 5th February, 1783, consisted of the Sovereign and twenty-two Knights, but now numbers only five Knights, no new Knights having been created since 1934. Investitures took place in the Cathedral of St. Patrick in Dublin. There is no special Chapel of the Order. The badge of the Order

FIG. 54. BADGE OF THE ORDER
OF ST. PATRICK.

pendant from the collar includes the saltire gules of St. Patrick surmounted by a trefoil charged with an imperial crown on each of its three leaves (Fig. 54).

4. THE MOST HONOURABLE ORDER OF THE BATH.

This Order was revived with great splendour by George I at the instigation of Sir Robert Walpole in 1725. It was instituted by Henry IV in 1399 and included the symbolic knightly act of bathing. At the revival in 1725 the Order in addition to the Sovereign, Great Master, and the infant Prince William (aged four) who later became the notorious Butcher of Culloden, consisted of thirty-five Knights only, but in the early part of the last century the Order was divided and enlarged into Military and Civil Divisions. The badge of the Order (Military Division) is a gold eight-pointed cross, enamelled in white, with a lion passant guardant within each angle, and in the centre the national emblems issuant from a sceptre between three imperial crowns within a red circle (Fig. 55). The badge of the Civil Division is of the same design within a circlet instead of a cross (Fig. 56). The Chapel of the Order, since 1725

FIG. 55.

FIG. 56.

BADGES OF THE ORDER OF THE BATH (MILITARY AND CIVIL DIVISIONS).

resplendent with banners, crests and stall plates, is that of Henry VII, Westminster Abbey (See also Chapter XVI).

5. THE MOST DISTINGUISHED ORDER OF ST. MICHAEL AND ST. GEORGE.

Instituted by George IV when Prince Regent on the 27th April, 1818, this Order commemorates the placing under British protection of the Republic of the Ionian Islands and is awarded for services to the Crown in the Imperial, Colonial and Diplomatic fields. The Order which has been much enlarged now consists of three classes, Knights Grand Cross, Knights Commanders and Companions. It consists of not more than 100 Knights Grand Cross, 300 Knights Commanders and 800 Companions. The badge, a cross of fourteen points, is of white enamel surmounted by an imperial crown with the figure of St. Michael in the centre trampling on Satan on one side and in the centre of the reverse side the figure of St. George. The Chapel of the Order is in St. Paul's Cathedral, resplendent with nineteen banners and a few stall plates (See Chapter XVI).

6. THE ROYAL VICTORIAN ORDER.

Her Majesty Queen Victoria instituted this Order on 21st April, 1896 as an award for important or personal services to the Sovereign. This Order has five classes, Knights Grand Cross, Dames Grand Cross, Knights Commanders, Dames Commanders, Commanders and Members 4th and 5th class. The badge is a white enamelled "Maltese" cross and on an oval centre the imperial cypher of Queen Victoria.

The Chapel of the Savoy has been the Chapel of the Order since 1938 and contains a superb collection of modern enamelled stall plates (See also Chapter XVI).

7. THE MOST EXCELLENT ORDER OF THE BRITISH EMPIRE.

This Order, founded by George V in June 1917, is awarded for important services to the Empire. It consists of five classes, Knights Grand Cross, Dames Grand Cross, Knights Commanders, Dames Commanders, Commanders, Officers and Members. The badge is a grey enamel cross patonce ensigned by the crown, bearing a gold medallion in the centre with the crowned effigies of King George and Queen Mary.

8. THE ORDER OF ST. JOHN OF JERUSALEM.

The first Crusade was responsible for the foundation of the ancient Order of the Hospital of St. John of Jerusalem frequently known as the Knights Hospitaller in contra-distinction to that other ancient Order of Chivalry the Knights Templar, both of which were founded by devout pilgrims for the recovery and the protection of the Holy Sepulchre. At the suppression of the Knights Templar by Edward II their property passed to the Knights of St. John and included the famous Temple property in London which was leased in turn to the "Students of the Law" who are still in possession.

The Order of St. John still continues its good work by carrying out the original intention of giving aid to the sick and wounded in times of peace and war. Probably the best known modern work of the Order is that of its Ambulance Department familiar to us all as the St. John Ambulance Brigade which was started in 1877. The badge of the Order is a white cross of eight points ornamented by a

FIG. 57.   BADGE OF THE ORDER
OF ST. JOHN OF JERUSALEM.

lion and unicorn alternately (Fig. 57). The Chapel of this Order is St. John, Clerkenwell, bombed early in 1941, but the gatehouse of the Priory nearby, built in 1504, remained unharmed. It has a richly vaulted archway emblazoned with shields of the arms of the Order renewed in 1893.

BARONETS AND KNIGHTS BACHELOR.

The title of Baronet is an hereditary rank below the peerage, created first by James I as a means of obtaining funds and colonizing Ulster, and for that reason a Baronet's badge portrays the red hand of Ulster on a small white shield and is used as an augmentation. There is a legend concerning this charge which is derived from the arms of the O'Neills whose ancestor won his Irish territory by cutting off his hand and flinging it to the shore in order to beat his companions in their race to touch land first.

A Knight Bachelor, the oldest form of Knighthood, is unattached to any Knightly Order. The badge of the Knight Bachelor only dates from 1926.

CHAPTER XIII

THE ROYAL ARMS

FROM the earliest days of Heraldry, the English Lions in the arms of the Sovereigns were referred to as the "Leopards of England". There were originally only two forms of lion in use in heraldic display:

1. The lion rampant, probably the oldest form of heraldic lion (Fig. 20A).
2. The lion passant guardant, which from the outset was termed a leopard (Fig. 20E).

As time went on the heraldic artists depicted the lion in various attitudes in order to provide a further variety of charges to cope with an increasing list of armigerous persons. The Royal Arms, however, have never altered or included any form of lion other than the first two mentioned already. For the benefit of the artist who would illustrate the heraldic lion it is essential that the characteristics as portrayed by the early armourists be preserved in the form of fierceness, simplicity of form and greyhound-like sleekness.

The fussiness and "pussycat" treatment of the eighteenth and nineteenth centuries (Fig. 34) are entirely out of keeping with the bold simplicity of design that heraldic art demands.

The illustrations in the early Rolls of Arms and the carvings on the tombs of the thirteenth century provide us with wonderful examples of the heraldic lion, so easily recognizable at a distance, a very important feature when the device was used as a rallying point in battle.

The present Royal Arms (Fig. 58) unchanged since Queen Victoria's accession, are blazoned; Quarterly 1 and 4 England, gules three lions passant guardant or, 2, Scotland or, a rampant lion within a double tressure fleury counter-fleury gules, 3 Ireland azure, a harp or, stringed argent.

The English quartering of the Arms was first used by Richard Coeur de Lion in 1198, the year in which he died, and the number

FIG. 58.

TO-DAY.

FIG. 59.

1340–1405.

THE ROYAL ARMS.

of lions, three, one above the other, were, like so many other devices of the period, almost certainly an allusion to the Holy Trinity.

Richard's second Great Seal of the Realm bore also the new shield—the three leopards of England. This shield was borne also by King John, Henry III, Edward I, Edward II and Edward III, then in the year 1340 (the year in which he styled himself King of France as well as of England) King Edward III added the beautiful fleurs de lys of France. He laid claim to the throne of France because his mother was the daughter of King Charles IV of France. Charles having died without male issue, the constitution of France prevented his daughter from acceding to the throne.

Edward III quartered the fleurs de lys with the leopards of England (Fig. 59) giving the fleurs de lys precedence to add weight to his claim. This French quartering bore the arms of France (ancient) azure, powdered with fleurs de lys, or; its ancient term is semee de lys, which indicates that the pattern on the background would appear to have been cut out of a larger sheet of design. A very fine example of these can be seen on an enamelled shield on the side of Edward III's tomb in Westminster Abbey. The Black Prince bore these arms too when he distinguished himself at Poictiers as can be seen on his effigy at Canterbury. This new Royal coat of arms came into being with the commencement of the

3

conflict we now know as The Hundred Years War between England and France.

This new quartering, however, had come to stay, for it was not abandoned until George III's reign—1801.

The Royal Arms continued in this form during the reign of Edward III's successor, Richard II, who was succeeded by Henry IV, the first of the Lancastrian Kings, in 1399, but in c. 1405 the French quartering was revised to conform to the design changed in France a quarter of a century earlier, azure three fleurs de lys or (Fig. 60). For close on two centuries c. 1405–1603 the Royal Arms of England remained unchanged and were as familiar to the followers of Joan of Arc as to the men of Henry V at Agincourt and Henry VIII on the splendid Field of the Cloth of Gold. The mariners of Sir Francis Drake aboard the *Golden Hind* and the sailors who fought under Sir Richard Grenville against the Spanish Armada, sailed under Elizabeth's flag blazoned with these arms.

In 1603, James VI of Scotland became James I of England, Scotland, France and Ireland, on the death of Queen Elizabeth. James was the first English Monarch to use the arms of the kingdom of Ireland. The Royal Arms were altered to conform to the new reigning house of Stuart by adding the Lion of Scotland and the Harp of Ireland as illustrated in Fig. 61.

His son, Charles I, and his grandsons, Charles II and James II, bore these arms until James II fled the country in 1688 and William

FIG. 60.

1405–1603.

FIG. 61.

1603–1688; 1702–1707.

FIG. 62.

FIG. 63.

1688–1702.

1707–1714.

of Orange came over to succeed him as William III. The arms of
Nassau were then added (azure, powdered billets and a lion or)
as an escutcheon on the centre of the shield (Fig. 62).

William was followed by Queen Anne in 1702 and for the early
part of her reign the Royal Arms of the Stuarts were once again
displayed until in 1706 the Act of Union with Scotland was passed.
The arms were then altered to show the merger (Fig. 63) England
and Scotland impaled, in the first and fourth quarters, France in the
second, and Ireland in the third quarter. The house of Stuart ceased
with the death of Queen Anne in 1714 and the accession of George I,
Elector of Hanover and a descendant of the grand-daughter of
James I of England, necessitated a further change in the arms to
incorporate the arms of the Electorate (Fig. 64) in the fourth quarter.
The arms on this quartering were as follows: Brunswick, gules two
leopards or, impaling Luneberg, or powdered with hearts gules
and a lion rampant azure, with a point in the base of the shield of
Westphalia gules, a running horse, argent. Overall on an escutcheon
gules, the crown of Charlemagne or, the symbol of the Elector's
office in the Holy Roman Empire.

With this addition the Arms remained during the reigns of
George I, George II and part of George III until 1801 when the
official union with Ireland came about, and the arms of France were
dropped. The arms were rearranged placing the arms of England
in the first and fourth quarters, Scotland in the second and Ireland

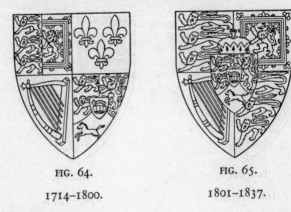

FIG. 64.   FIG. 65.

1714–1800.   1801–1837.

in the third, whilst the arms of Hanover were borne on an in-escutcheon in the centre of the shield surmounted by the Elector's gules and ermine cap (Fig. 65) only to be altered in 1815 when the Electorate of Hanover became a kingdom and the cap was changed to a crown. The arms continued in this amended form for the re-mainder of George III's reign and remained in use during the reign of his successors, George IV and William IV.

William died in 1837 and was succeeded by his niece Princess Victoria, the only child of William's brother Edward, Duke of Kent.

Queen Victoria was not eligible under the laws of Hanover to succeed to the kingdom of Hanover and so the arms of Hanover were removed from the Royal Arms. These arms (Fig. 58) have remained unchanged since that time, having been used successively by Edward VII, George V, Edward VIII, George VI, and now by Her Majesty Queen Elizabeth II. The supporters to the Royal Arms as illustrated (Fig. 69) have remained unchanged since the reign of James I.

The Royal Arms in Scotland.

From the time of James I (1603) it has been the practice to marshal the Royal Arms as used in Scotland, giving precedence to the Scot-tish quarter and the unicorn supporter regally crowned.

The Royal Arms as allowed to be displayed on the Great Seal of Scotland are shown in Fig. 66 "the ruddy lion ramping in his

FIG. 66.

THE ROYAL ARMS
IN SCOTLAND.

field of gold" occupying the first and fourth quarters in place of the
leopards of England which have been given second place in the next
quarter. In addition there is the personal achievement of the Sovereign,
as King of Scotland, of the tressured lion alone which is the exclusive
property of the sovereign.

This chapter would not be complete without reference to the
arms of the Duke of Edinburgh, and Queen Elizabeth, the Queen
Mother.

His Royal Highness the Duke of Edinburgh bears for arms
(Fig. 67) the four quarterings of Denmark, Greece, Mountbatten
and the City of Edinburgh. The supporters consist of Hercules

FIG. 67.

ARMS OF H.R.H.
THE DUKE OF
EDINBURGH.

FIG. 68. ARMS OF THE QUEEN MOTHER.

from his Greek Royal Arms, and the Hesse Lion gorged with a naval crown in allusion to his association with the Senior Service.

The arms of the Queen Mother (Fig. 68) are those of the Sovereign impaling Bowes Lyon.

Her Majesty's Stationery Office (H.M.S.O.) use the Royal Arms on their many official publications, a very fine modern design, as illustrated in Fig. 69.

FIG. 69. THE ROYAL ARMS (H.M.S.O.)

CHAPTER XIV

CIVIC, ECCLESIASTIC, COLLEGIATE AND CORPORATE HERALDRY

ARMORIAL Bearings have been granted by the Heralds to Civic Bodies since the sixteenth century, although as early as the fourteenth century seals bearing the arms of English cities were known.

Nowadays every city and nearly every town possesses its coat of arms displayed on municipal buildings and vehicles alike, for civic bodies during the last half century have become alive to the value and beauty of heraldry and many who possessed irregular coats of arms have now had these arms regularized and recorded by the College of Arms. There are still, however, some London Boroughs who have not yet put their house in order.

The City of London.

Oddly enough there is no evidence that the very ancient arms of the City were ever granted although the shield was certainly in use at least a century before the Incorporation of the College of Arms (1484) which recognizes the authenticity of the Arms, argent, a cross and in the first quarter a sword in pale, point uppermost, gules. The now famous dragon supporters were not added until 1633 and were supposed to allude to the legend of St. George, the patron saint of England, whose cross is borne on the city shield. The sword, that of St. Paul (and not as some have it the dagger of Wat Tyler) symbolizes not only the great masterpiece of Sir Christopher Wren but also its seventh-century predecessor. The helmet supporting the dragon wing crest is that of a Peer, for the office of Lord Mayor of London ranks with the Peerage (Fig. 70).

City of York.

The arms of the City of York, said to be over 500 years old, were certainly recorded by Robert Glover, Somerset Herald, in 1584 and are argent, on a cross gules, five lions passant guardant or (Fig. 71). This very interesting as well as ancient coat contains the Cross of St. George as well as the Leopards of England.

FIG. 70.

ARMS OF THE CITY OF LONDON.

FIG. 71.

ARMS OF THE CITY OF YORK.

Beckenham, Kent.

As a contrast from the ancient shields of London and York, Fig. 72 illustrates the modern coat of the Borough of Beckenham in the County of Kent granted in 1931, with the addition of supporters in 1935. The arms are vert two bars wavy argent between as many chestnut trees in full blossom and eradicated proper in chief and a horse forcene (rampant) argent in base. For the Crest on a Wreath of the Colours a demi lion guardant or, supporting a pastoral staff argent enfiled with a mitre proper, and for the supporters on the dexter side a gentleman and on the sinister side a lady both in the costume of the early sixteenth century.

The general colour scheme of the shield is green. This is suggestive of the Beckenham of old, a township with a rural setting.

The chestnut trees in bloom (unique, probably in civic heraldry) are in keeping with this idea and are indicative of the beauty of the flowering shrubs and trees in many parts of the town during spring and summer, and of the parks and well-wooded gardens. The wavy lines form a symbol of the River Beck which, though actually only a stream, has given the town its name. Below is the white horse of Kent, linking up Beckenham with one of the most famous counties of England.

FIG. 72. ARMS OF THE
BOROUGH OF BECKENHAM,
KENT.

For a crest, reference has been made to the ancient and modern ownership of large areas of Beckenham. The lion is the lion of the Cator Family, and the ecclesiastical symbols in its grasp are representative of Bishop Odo, of Bayeux; he was half-brother to William the Conqueror, who presented the land and manors of Beckenham to the Bishop.

The supporters are indicative of outstanding features in the story of Beckenham (which now of course embraces the major part of West Wickham, including the historic Wickham Court), namely, its interesting Tudor associations.

The motto—a Ciceronian phrase—proclaims the principle "Not for ourselves alone."

Ecclesiastical Heraldry.

The close of the thirteenth century saw the assumption of arms by the great monastic houses, the clergy in general following the nobility by sealing their documents with the seals of the arms of their houses. The arms of bishops are surmounted by a mitre. A crest, helmet and motto are never used in this instance, although the Bishop of Durham displays a mitre issuing from a coronet, a reminder of his one-time Palatine jurisdiction.

Archbishops and bishops of dioceses impale their personal arms with those of their Sees. The arms of the See on the dexter side.

A cardinal surmounts his arms with his scarlet hat with fifteen tassels on either side (Fig. 73).

FIG. 73.

CARDINAL'S HAT.

SEES IN THE PROVINCE OF CANTERBURY

Canterbury. Azure, an archbishop's crozier (staff silver and cross gold) surmounted by a pall in its proper colours. (Fig. 74.)

London. Gules, two swords (St. Paul) or, crossed saltire-wise, points upwards.

FIG. 74.

ARMS OF THE ARCHBISHOP OF CANTERBURY.

Winchester. Gules, St. Peter's keys, gold and silver with the sword of St. Paul between them saltirewise, blade silver, hilt gold.

Bangor. Gules, a bend or, sprinkled with sable drops between two mullets pierced, argent.

Bath and Wells. Azure, a saltire quartered saltirewise or and argent.

Birmingham. Party indented or and gules five roundels with two crosses forming in chief, all counterchanged.

Bristol. Sable, three crowns in pale or.

Chichester. Azure, the figure of Our Lord in white seated on a gold throne, and issuing from his mouth fesswise, a sword, blade argent and hilt or.

Ely. Gules, three crowns or.

Exeter. Gules, a sword argent, point uppermost, surmounted by two keys in saltire or.

Gloucester. Azure, two keys in saltire or.

Hereford. Gules three fleurs de lys issuing from three leopards' faces, or.

Lichfield. Party gules and argent, a cross potent and quadrate in the centre between four crosslets patee, all counterchanged.

Lincoln. Gules two lions passant guardant or, on a chief azure the Holy Virgin and Child crowned and bearing a sceptre, or.

Llandaff. Sable, two croziers saltirewise, one or, the other argent, on a chief azure, three mitres, or.

Norwich. Azure, three mitres or.

Oxford. Sable, a fess argent between in chief three ladies' heads affronte arrayed argent and crowned or, in base an ox argent passing over a ford proper.

Peterborough. Gules, St. Peter's keys saltirewise between four crosslets fitchy or.

Rochester. Argent, on a saltire gules a scallop shell or.

St. Albans. Azure, a saltire or, overall a sword, blade argent, hilt or, point uppermost with a celestial crown over the point.

St. Asaph. Sable, two keys saltirewise argent.

St. Davids. Sable, a cross or, thereon five cinquefoils sable.

Salisbury. Azure the Holy Virgin with Child or.

Southwark. Argent, a cross indented with a mitre gules, in the first quarter.

Southwell. Sable, three fountains proper, a chief or, thereon a pale, azure charged with the Holy Virgin and Child, between on the dexter a stag lodged proper and on the sinister side two staves ragully, crossed, vert.

Truro. Argent upon saltire gules a key, ward uppermost surmounted by a sword hilt uppermost or, in base a fleur de lys sable, all within a border sable charged with fifteen bezants.

Worcester. Argent, ten roundels gules.

SEES IN THE PROVINCE OF YORK

York. Gules two keys saltirewise argent and in chief a crown or.

Durham. Azure a cross or between four lions rampant argent.

Carlisle. Argent a cross sable with a mitre or, thereon.

Chester. Gules three mitres, or.

Liverpool. Argent, the eagle of St. John holding an inkhorn sable. On a chief parted azure and gules an open book having on its leaves the words "Thy word is Truth" on the dexter and on the sinister side a three-masted ship, or.

Manchester. Or, on a pale engrailed gules three mitres, and a quarter gules with three bends enhanced, or.

Newcastle. Gules, three castles argent and a chief azure with the golden cross of St. Cuthbert thereon.

Ripon. Argent on a saltire gules, two keys in saltire or, on a chief gules, one pascal lamb proper.

Sodor and Man. Gules, upon a pedestal the Holy Virgin arms extended between two pillars, in her dexter hand a church, and in base three legs in armour conjoined in fess.

Wakefield. Gules, a fleur de lys or, and a chief azure with three celestial crowns or thereon.

Collegiate Arms.

At their inception the Colleges of both Oxford and Cambridge were religious houses, for their Masters and Fellows were Clerks in Holy Orders and they were therefore subject to a statute enacting every religious house to have a common seal. These seals for the most part displayed the arms of the founders and benefactors and from this early source came the arms of the Colleges.

The arms of the University of Oxford (Fig. 75), dating from the middle of the fifteenth century, are: azure a book proper leathered gules, garnished or, having on its dexter side seven gold seals, the words DOMINUS ILLUMINATIO MEA, between three open crowns proper. The arms of the University of Cambridge, granted to William Cecil, Lord Burghley, the Chancellor of the University

FIG. 75.

ARMS OF THE
UNIVERSITY OF
OXFORD.

on 8th June, 1573, are gules, on a cross ermine between four lions
passant guardant or a book gules.

Corporate Heraldry.

The use of Heraldry by our national Institutions and learned
Societies is fairly widespread and there is no doubt that a coat of
arms adds lustre to their publications. Figure 76 illustrates the arms
of the Institution of Electrical Engineers, azure, within an annulet
flory, at the four cardinal points a winged thunderbolt or; on a
chief barry wave azure and or, an open book proper garnished gules,
on the leaves therefore the words DISCE DOCE in letters sable. And
for the crest, on a wreath of the colours a leopard statant or, supporting in his dexter fore-paw a caduceus of the same; as supporters,
on a compartment vert, two pegasi argent, crined unguled and
winged or, each charged on the breast with a St. Michael's cross gules.

The shield shows in the upper part, or chief, a pattern of blue and

FIG. 76.

ARMS OF THE INSTITUTION
OF ELECTRICAL ENGINEERS.

gold waves, representing one of the fundamental concepts of electrical engineering, on which an open book appears bearing the words DISCE DOCE—learn and teach—an allusion to the benefits derived from the exchange of knowledge as well as to the interest of The Institution in engineering education.

The lower part of the shield shows a background of blue—by common consent the predominantly "electrical" colour—on which a winged golden thunderbolt appears, enclosed in a golden ring bearing golden fleurs de lys at the four cardinal points. This alludes to the power of electricity circumscribed and under control; the fleurs de lys on the encircling ring make a passing reference to the compass card. Here the Royal leopard stands on a wreath and mantle in which the principal colours of the shield are repeated, supported by a squire's helm, marking the status of The Institution as a body incorporated by Royal Charter. The leopard supports in his right fore-paw the caduceus, or winged staff of Mercury, symbol of communication, since Mercury was the Messenger of the Gods.

The Royal leopard signifies the source of The Institution's authority in the Crown, and the caduceus alludes both to the important place of electrical communication in the interests of The Institution and to its original foundation, in 1871, as The Society of Telegraph Engineers.

The Supporters. The presence of supporters in the full representation of the arms is another mark of the corporate status of The Institution. The two white, winged horses, or pegasi, are chosen to represent speed and docility, qualities well in keeping with electricity in the service of man. To prevent confusion with the bearers of other coats of arms in which pegasi appear as supporters, a mark of difference is applied to them, in this case the St. Michael's cross on their breasts, thus making an indirect allusion to the interest and pride of The Institution in Michael Faraday and his work.

The *Radio Times* proudly displays the arms of the B.B.C. on the heading of its title-page.

The following Armorial Bearings, Supporters and Badge were granted and assigned to The British Broadcasting Corporation under Letters Patent dated the 8th day of March 1927.

Arms. Azure, a terrestrial globe proper encircled by an annulet or and seven estoiles in orle—argent.

Crest. On a wreath of the colours a lion passant or grasping in the dexter fore-paw a thunderbolt proper.

Supporters. On either side an eagle, wings addorsed—proper collared azure pendant therefrom a bugle horn stringed or.

Badge. A thunderbolt proper thereon a pellet inscribed with the letters B.B.C. in gold.

Mottoes. Nation shall speak peace unto nation or "Quaecunque". (Fig. 77).

FIG. 77. ARMS OF THE BRITISH BROADCASTING CORPORATION.

The Royal Society founded by Royal Charter in 1662 is privileged to use part of the Royal Arms in its coat of arms, a rare example indeed. The arms are argent, on a quarter gules the three leopards of England.

The Performing Rights Society possess a unique coat of arms, granted in recent years and embodying a conductor's baton and a musical stave, whilst the crest, a swan, no doubt taken from the arms of the Worshipful Company of Musicians, alludes to the swan in mythology, sacred to Apollo, god of Fine Arts.

CHAPTER XV

HERALDRY IN COMMERCE

THE formation of the Worshipful Companies of the City of London gave a sense of dignity as well as of importance to the merchants who became members, and from all the companies formed the Hudson's Bay Company alone survives as a commercial corporation. Grants of arms were made to these companies, that of the Drapers as early as 1439. Many of them bear the devices of the trades with which they were concerned as, for instance, the arms of the Grocers Company, argent a chevron gules between nine cloves sable, and that of the Vintners—sable, a chevron between three tuns (casks) argent. The banners of some of these companies are often carried in the Lord Mayor's Show.

During the Festival of Britain, flags bearing the arms of the City Companies were flown from the new corporation garden at the south-eastern corner of St. Paul's Cathedral. The arms of these companies are familiar to all the scholars past and present of the famous schools endowed by members as well as by the companies themselves; to name but a few, the Mercers, the Clothworkers, the Haberdashers and the Goldsmiths.

Trading bodies were formed to co-operate with the City Companies, the Merchant Adventurers being an excellent example, founded by the Mercers Company, and these in turn have been joined by the great Banking and Insurance Houses, which because of their national importance have also been granted coats of arms.

Barclays Bank.

Grant of Arms dated 22nd October, 1937: "Argent an eagle displayed sable charged on the body and on each wing with a Ducal Coronet of the field." (Fig. 78.)

The sign of the black spread eagle has been associated with the Bank for more than three centuries, although its origin is uncertain. It was hanging in Lombard Street at least from the late seventeenth century, for the first reference to it appeared in the London Gazette

FIG. 78.

EAGLE FROM THE ARMS
OF BARCLAYS BANK.

in 1676 when the premises No. 56 were occupied by a goldsmith named James Taylor, who advertised for a runaway boy. By 1728 Messrs. Freame and Gould, goldsmiths, were the occupants, and when in that year John Freame started the business which was in the passage of time to become Barclays Bank, he retained the sign. In 1937 a coat of arms was granted the Bank, in which the black spread eagle and another ancient Lombard Street sign—that of the three crowns—were incorporated.

(The history of the sign of the three crowns is not known, apart from the belief that it identified No. 43 Lombard Street, the site of which is also covered by the present Head Office of the Bank. However, Hilton Price in *The Signs of Old Lombard Street*, identifies No. 7 as well as No. 43 with this sign, and it is possible therefore that Barclays Bank has no claim to it.)

The National Coal Board acquired a grant of arms (Fig. 79) in 1949. Per fess, argent and sable three fusils conjoined in fess counterchanged. The charge on this shield consists of an heraldic pattern which symbolizes the raising of coal from beneath the surface of the ground, whilst the lion supporters represent Britain and the sun on each shoulder signifies the products of coal, heat, light and power. This grant with its motto "E Tenebris Lux" (Light out of Darkness) moved the Press to some good-natured comment at the time.

The Gas Council, too, has its coat of arms on which a flame appears, signifying gas, whilst the background is black signifying

FIG. 79. ARMS OF THE NATIONAL COAL BOARD.

coal, the whole within a border on which are portrayed twelve annulets (rings) to represent the twelve Area Boards.

Scottish Airlines. This grant of arms (Fig. 80) carrying the crowned heart of Douglas is to be seen painted on the sides of the aircraft flown regularly by Scottish Airlines to and from Prestwick. Granted by the Lord Lyon King of Arms in April 1945, to Scottish Aviation, the parent body, the grant of arms reads as follows:

"To ALL AND SUNDRY whom these presents do or may concern, We, Sir Francis James Grant, Knight Commander of the Royal Victorian Order, Doctor of Laws, Lord Lyon King of Arms, Send Greeting:—Whereas SCOTTISH AVIATION Limited, Prestwick Airport in the County of Ayr, hath by petition unto us of date the sixth day of April current shewn that Scottish Aviation Limited, Aircraft Constructors, Aeronautical Engineers and Airport Owners is a Company incorporated under the Companies Act (1929) for the purpose of furthering all branches of Aviation in Scotland for which purpose, on land purchased at Prestwick an Airport was constructed known as Prestwick Airport, AND the Petitioners having prayed that We would grant our Licence and Authority unto the said Scottish Aviation Limited to bear and use such Ensigns Armorial as might be found suitable and according to the Laws of Arms, KNOW Ye, therefore, that We

FIG. 80. ARMS OF SCOTTISH AVIATION LIMITED.

have devised and do by these presents Assign, Ratify and Confirm unto the said Scottish Aviation Limited the following Ensigns Armorial, as depicted upon the margin hereof and matriculated of even date with these presents upon the thirty-sixth folio of the thirty-fifth volume of Our Public Register of All Arms and Bearings in Scotland, videlicet: Argent, a demilion erased Azure, armed and langued gules, having wing coverts of the last feathered Or, in canton the Douglas heart imperially crowned proper (having reference to His Grace the Duke of Hamilton, Chairman of the said Company). Above the shield is placed an helmet of befitting Degree with Mantling Azure doubled Argent and on a Wreath of the Liveries is set for Crest:—within a circlet, Or, fimbriated Argent and winged fessways as the Arms, on a field Sable a Bengal tiger's face proper. On a Compartment semee of thistles below the shield, along with the motto 'THE WORLD O'ER' are set for Supporters:—two lions Azure armed and langued gules, and winged as the Arms. In Testimony whereof These Presents are Subscribed by Us and the Seal of Our Office is affixed hereto at Edinburgh the seven-

teenth day of April in the ninth year of the Reign of Our
Sovereign Lord George the Sixth, by the Grace of God, of Great
Britain, Ireland and the British Dominions beyond the Seas,
King, Defender of the Faith, Emperor of India, etc. and in the
year of Our Lord One thousand nine hundred and forty-five."

The crowned heart taken from the arms is also used as a cap
badge by the aircrew of Scottish Airlines.

THE ROYAL WARRANT HOLDERS

This association incorporated by Royal Charter in 1907 super-
vises the use of Royal Warrants to members of firms only who
supply the Royal Households with their products.

The warrants, signed by the Lord Chamberlain, are granted by
the Board of the Green Cloth, at Buckingham Palace, and this
privilege entitles the holders to display the Royal Arms with the
addition of the wording "By Royal Appointment to . . ." on the
shop fascia or notepaper of their business. (Fig. 81).

FIG. 81.

ROYAL ARMS AS
USED BY THE
ROYAL WARRANT
HOLDERS.

The appointment is rarely granted if the firm making the appli-
cation has not supplied the Royal Household for at least three years.
The appointment is renewed, subject to the holder maintaining the
very high standard of workmanship which qualified him for the
original warrant.

CHAPTER XVI

FLAGS, BANNERS, STANDARDS, STALL PLATES AND MONUMENTAL BRASSES

*"The great Standard to be sette before the
Kinges pavilion or tent, not to be borne
in battel, to be of the length of two yards."*

FROM time immemorial men at arms have carried before their armies a standard either carved in wood or metal, or painted or sewn on material. William the Conqueror was presented with a white banner by the Pope before setting off to do battle with Harold. Flags or Standards served as rallying points even in modern times.

Our own Union Flag, first used in 1801, is composed of three religious banners superimposed, and as every Boy Scout who has passed his tenderfoot knows, comprises the Red Cross of St. George, the white saltire (diagonal cross) on blue for St. Andrew and the red saltire on white for St. Patrick, though the latter is really the arms of the Fitzgeralds. The union flag is blazoned as follows:

Azure, the crosses saltire St. Andrew and St. Patrick quarterly, per saltire counterchanged argent and gules: the latter fimbriated (edged) argent, surmounted by the cross of St. George gules, fimbriated as the saltires.

Heraldic flags of the Church may be seen flying from time to time from the summit of the north-west tower of Westminster Abbey.

Flags should really be square like the heraldic banners, their forerunners.

Henry V displayed a banner of his arms at Agincourt just as to-day wherever Her Majesty stays the Royal Standard flies to denote her presence.

The same rules on tinctures apply to flags as to shields of arms. The very early banners were larger in depth than in width (Fig. 82), whilst the present day flags are just the opposite to the great detri-

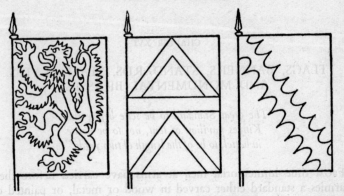

FIG. 82. EARLY HERALDIC BANNERS.

ment of their charges. The square banners of Knighthood at Windsor, Westminster and St. Paul's are correct.

Standards came into use in the fourteenth century (Edward III) and were borne in the great State funeral processions. The ancient standards always bore the cross of St. George, the motto, badge and crest of the bearer, but never the arms. Fig. 83 illustrates the standard of the County Council of the West Riding of Yorkshire (1927) and it will be noticed that the arms of the Council are used instead of the cross of St. George. The border is of the livery colours.

FIG. 83. HERALDIC STANDARD.

Standards are no longer granted to civic bodies.

The Standard is an elongated tapering flag sometimes split at the ends, Royal Standards excepted.

The Guydon resembles the standard in form and is less by one-third and generally terminates in a point.

The Pennon, half the size of the guydon, is charged only with the arms.

The Pencel or Pennoncelle is a diminutive of the pennon and was borne at the end of a lance, charged with either a crest or a device. (Fig. 84).

FIG. 84. STANDARD AND PENNONS.

STALL PLATES

St. George's Chapel, Windsor Castle.

Affixed to the panelling at the back of the choir stalls in St. George's Chapel, Windsor Castle, are about 700 gilded metal plates, bearing both enamelled and painted armorial ensigns dated from 1421 until the present day. These are known as Stall Plates and they commemorate the Knights of the Most Noble Order of the Garter, for although the banners which are suspended above the stalls are removed on the death of the Knight whose arms they bear, the stall plates remain in position in perpetuity. Despite the vicissitudes of time, there still remain above 42 per cent of the whole possible number. The present Chapel of the Order was sufficiently completed in 1483 to allow the use of the choir, and the stalls on which these plates appear were made between 1478 and 1483. The earlier stall plates were removed from the first chapel, which is now the Albert Memorial Chapel, to their present position although in the course of time some have been stolen, some removed on the degradation of a Knight, and some of course were never put up, which would account for the difference between the total of the Knights created as compared with the stall plates which remain. Three plates have been stolen since 1749. Some of the earlier plates commemorate the founder members of the Order, men who fought with the Black Prince, although strangely enough there are no plates in existence which commemorate either King Edward III or his son.

The Sovereign of the Order, as such, never has a stall plate, although fifteen of our sovereigns are commemorated by plates placed here on their elevation to the Order prior to their coming to the throne. There is one exception. A stall plate to Charles I, which was restored to the Chapel in 1950. The late Dr. Fellowes, Minor Canon of Windsor, who chanted the daily services in the Chapel for over fifty years until his death in December 1951, wrote "that as recently as 1928 a stall plate came to light with a good claim to be the lost stall plate of King Charles I. It was replaced in the stalls by desire of His Majesty, King George VI, and can be seen on the south side in the stall next but one to that occupied by the Sovereign." The ladies of the Order do not have stall plates. Figure 85 illustrates the stall plate of Richard Beauchamp, Earl of Warwick 1403-49. The arms are quarterly 1 and 4 gules, a fesse and six cross crosslets or (Beauchamp) 2 and 3, Chequey gold and azure a chevron ermine (for Newburgh) with an escutcheon of pretence quarterly 1 and 4 or three chevrons gules (for Clare) 2 and 3 quarterly argent, and gules fretty or, a bend sable (for Despencer). *The plate must have been made shortly after* 1423.

Westminster Abbey.

The stall plates of the Most Honourable Order of the Bath are affixed to the stalls in Henry VII's Chapel, Westminster Abbey, the earliest plates dating from the revival of the Order in 1725. These early engraved and enamelled brass plates may be seen on the back boards below the seats of the stalls, where they have been moved

FIG. 85. STALL PLATE — ST. GEORGE'S CHAPEL, WINDSOR CASTLE.

at some time to make room for the modern stall plates. On the panelling in front of the Dean's stall in the south-western corner are three modern enamelled plates of the Deans of Westminster showing the arms of the Abbey impaling their personal arms surrounded with the circle and motto of the Order. The more modern stall plates are very fine indeed, but the earlier plates are disappointing and have experienced harsh treatment, most of their original colouring having disappeared.

The Queen's Chapel of the Savoy.

The ancient Chapel of the Savoy just off the Strand in London contains a superb collection of modern stall plates in bronze and enamel, affixed to the oak panelling on three sides of the Chapel. The plates number sixty-seven. In the Sovereign's stalls are the stall plates of King George VI and Elizabeth the Queen Mother, whilst in the adjoining stalls are the stall plates of Queen Mary, Princess Louise and Princess Beatrice with their arms within a lozenge.

St. Paul's Cathedral.

The Chapel of the Distinguished Order of St. Michael and St. George is in the south-west corner of St. Paul's Cathedral and contains some very beautifully embroidered heraldic banners, a few enamelled stall plates and in the centre of the floor a group of memorial metal lozenge-shaped engraved achievements. There are twenty-one stalls in the Chapel reserved for Knights Grand Cross of the Order. At the time of writing there are nineteen banners hung over these stalls. When a stall holder dies, his vacant stall is offered to the next Knight Grand Cross in seniority who, before he can accept it, must be prepared to have a banner with his arms embroidered on it hung over the stall. If a Knight Grand Cross wishes to have a stall plate only, this is affixed to the side panel in the Chapel and the stall is offered to another.

Services are held annually in the Chapel when the banner of any deceased Knight is taken down, and the banner of the succeeding holder to the vacant stall is affixed in its place.

The reason for the small number of stall plates is that Knights Grand Cross who accept the privilege of having a stall need not have both a banner and a plate.

The practice of allowing memorial plates in the Chapel (there are a few on the centre of the chapel floor) was discontinued because of limited space.

St. Giles' Cathedral, Edinburgh.

There are very few stall plates in the Chapel of the Order of the Thistle because the Order is small and very exclusive. Those that are secured to the backs of the stalls are, of course, modern, since the Chapel dates from 1911 when it was dedicated in the presence of George V. They have a style quite their own and are interesting in comparison with the Garter, Bath, and the very modern Royal Victorian Order plates in the Savoy Chapel.

MONUMENTAL BRASSES

At the time of the Dissolution of the Monasteries about 150,000 floor brasses were known to exist in England, of which not more than a third can be found to-day. Many still remain in their original positions on the floors of our churches and are usually protected by matting or carpet, whilst those which were moved to make way for modern flooring were for the most part inserted in the walls nearby. These monumental brass plates were first used in this country in the thirteenth century, the earliest remaining example being at Stoke D'Abernon Church, Surrey (Fig. 86) to commemorate Sir John D'Abernon. Heraldry plays a great part in the designs, in some places as isolated coats of arms, in others on the heraldic surcoats, quite a large proportion contain groups of shields of arms and many still retain their original enamelling.

FIG. 86.

MONUMENTAL
BRASS.

In Scotland where there have never been many brasses, the famous brass to the Regent Moray, half brother to Mary, Queen of Scots, is to be seen in St. Giles' Cathedral, Edinburgh. This contains his coat of arms indicating his Royal descent. He was assassinated on 23rd January, 1569, and the memorial brass dates from 1570.

Another plate, but in this instance of copper, was and may still be in the churchyard at Kilmany, Fifeshire, and contains eight shields. The plate commemorates John Melville of Cairnie and dates from 1794.

CHAPTER XVII

THE HERALDS, COLLEGE OF ARMS, AND COURT OF THE LORD LYON

"Herald, read the accusation!" said the King.
On this the White Rabbit blew three blasts
on the trumpet."

Alice in Wonderland.

So wrote Lewis Carroll in the story which has delighted children of all ages since 1865. Heralds in reality are not State Trumpeters, but their proclamations are certainly preceded and followed by a fanfare from the trumpeters of the Household Cavalry.

The duties of the Heralds go back to the days of the first tournaments. Just as the referee at a boxing contest to-day proclaims the style of the contestants, so the Heralds in their early days proclaimed the contesting knights in the tiltyard.

Their duties included that of conveying messages and peace offerings abroad in addition to the control over the use of coat armour, and the arranging of the heraldry of warfare.

Rouge Croix and York Herald were used to discharge messages at the Fatal Field of Flodden as was the Scottish Herald, Islay. It was of the utmost importance that they should be well learned in the art of heraldry to enable them to conduct their periodic "visitations" to register and correct the illegal assumption of arms.

To-day the duties of the Heralds are concerned with the marshalling of state ceremonies (the coronation, the opening of Parliament, and the funeral of the Sovereign), attending Court functions, recording and registering grants of arms and in the case of the Kings of Arms granting new arms where applications have been approved, and incidentally anyone can apply for a grant of arms.

The Earl Marshal, an office devolving by heredity upon the Dukes of Norfolk, is the official head of the College of Arms.

The corporation of the College consists of three Kings of Arms, six Heralds and four Pursuivants.

Kings of Arms.

Garter Principal King of Arms was originally created by Henry V in 1415 to deal with the ceremonies of the Order of the Garter. The arms of his office are argent, a cross gules, on a chief azure, a coronet encircled with the Garter between a lion passant guardant and a fleur de lys, or. (Fig. 87.)

FIG. 87.

ARMS OF THE GARTER
KING OF ARMS.

Norroy, whose province is north of the Trent (Roi du Nord), is the oldest office, the title going back to Edward III.

Clarenceaux, whose province is south of the Trent, takes his title from Clare in Suffolk, from whence the Royal title of Clarence was also taken.

An Ireland King of Arms appears from the time of Richard II until the reign of Edward IV. The office was revived under a new title of Ulster by Edward VI, which continued up to the time of the formation of the Irish Republic when the office was combined with that of Norroy.

The Irish Genealogical Office in Dublin Castle now deals with all Heraldry in Southern Ireland and has at its head the Chief Herald of Ireland.

Heralds.

Of the many titles given to Heralds since their creation only six survive, and these are Windsor, York, Lancaster, Chester, Richmond and Somerset. Edward III created Windsor, named after the Castle, York and Lancaster after his two sons, and Chester after the City.

Richmond was created by Edward IV and Henry VIII created Somerset after his illegitimate son Henry Fitzroy, Duke of Somerset.

Pursuivants.

The four Pursuivants are Rouge Croix named after the Cross of St. George, Bluemantle probably from the blue robes of the Order of the Garter (Edward III), Rouge Dragon from one of the supporters of Henry VII's arms, and lastly Portcullis from· one of Henry VII's badges.

Heralds Extraordinary and Pursuivants are sometimes made without the holders becoming members of the College.

Official Dress.

The tabard is illustrated in Fig. 2 and is worn by all Officers of Arms over uniforms. It is emblazoned with the Royal Arms of the Sovereign, the tabard of the Kings of Arms being of velvet, that of the Herald of satin, whilst that of the Pursuivant is of damask silk.

The Kings of Arms wear their crowns at coronations only.

The College of Arms.

The site on which the present building in Queen Victoria Street stands was granted by Mary Tudor on 18th July, 1554. Prior to this date it had been the town house of the Earls of Derby. The building was destroyed in 1666 during the fire of London, and rebuilt in the style of Sir Christopher Wren by Morris Emmott, the King's builder, in 1677, and is standing to-day despite the war scars around it. Fortunately, it has suffered very little damage. The entrance was formerly in Godliman Street, the keystone only remains now to remind us of the alterations made when Queen Victoria Street was constructed in the latter part of the last century.

The Earl Marshal's Court, approached by a double flight of steps, is still as portrayed by Rowlandson and Pugin in their drawings for *The Microcosm of London*, published in 1808.

The beautifully embroidered banners carried at the coronation service of King George VI are hanging over the panelling of this very handsome Court room, whilst the Earl Marshal's throne within an oak rail is surmounted by the arms of Queen Anne.

The arms of the College (Fig. 88) are blazoned: argent, a cross gules, between four doves their dexter wings elevated and inverted azure.

FIG. 88. ARMS OF THE COLLEGE OF ARMS.

Crest. On a ducal coronet or, a dove rising azure.
Supporters. Two lions rampant guardant azure, ducally gorged or.

THE SCOTTISH HERALDS

The Lyon Court.
The Lord Lyon King of Arms whose title is derived from
the rampant lion in the Scottish Royal Arms, is not an official
within the department of the Earl Marshal but derives his
authority from the Office of Chronicles (Sennachie) of the Celtic
Kings. He was given control of Heraldry in the thirteenth
century, but the title Lord Lyon dates from the early sixteenth
century. As one of the Officers of State in Scotland, and a Judge of
the Realm, he is also King of Arms of the Order of the Thistle;
he has authority to examine, control and reform by erasure if
necessary, and to impose fines and other penalties where arms are
irregularly used, the arms and armorial ensigns of all Scottish peers
and gentlemen or Corporate bodies, and to grant arms "to all
virtuous and well deserving persons" who may apply for them.
He is the chief authority on genealogy in Scotland, and his rulings
include the Chiefship of families and Headship of Clans.

The arms of Lord Lyon are: argent, a lion sejant erect and
affronte gules holding in his dexter paw a thistle slipped vert and
in the sinister a shield gules on a chief azure a St. Andrew's saltire.
(Fig. 89.)

FIG. 89. ARMS OF LYON KING OF ARMS.

The supporters date from the early seventeenth century. The two batons behind the arms differ; one is the Lyon Baton, the other the Thistle Staff. The crown surmounting the arms is the old Lyon crown, similar to the crown of Scotland, but with the circlet enamelled azure.

There are fewer basic coats of arms in Scotland because there are fewer surnames, half the population being correlated in the great Highland Clans. In 1672 an Act of Parliament ordered that nobody should use arms in Scotland that were not properly matriculated in the Lyon Register, which, like the Register of Genealogies, is a "Public Register of the Kingdom". These and the Lyon Court Books are part of the national records of Scotland.

Accordingly, the Court of the Lord Lyon is situate in Her Majesty's Register House, Edinburgh. Arms in Scotland are Ensigns of Noblesse and the procedure for establishing right to them is judicial, so the petitioner gets a judicial decree of his noblesse and pedigree. In Court, the Lord Lyon still on solemn occasions wears the velvet and ermine robe such as he wore at the olden Scottish coronations. There are three Heralds under the Lord Lyon, namely: Marchmont, Albany, and Rothesay. The earliest named in record is Marchmont, 1436, Albany, 1452, and Rothesay, 1491.

The three Pursuivants are Carrick, Unicorn and Kintyre. Carrick (1365) is the earliest mentioned under his title. Falkland and Linlithgow are Pursuivants-Extraordinary occasionally in commission.

CHAPTER XVIII

SEE FOR YOURSELF

THIS small volume would be incomplete without a guide, brief though it must be, to some of the outstanding examples both ancient and modern of armorial designs in Britain. Parish church and cathedral alike are our treasure houses for this form of traditional art, whilst the British Museum, the Victoria and Albert Museum, and the Museum of the Public Record Office, contain superb collections. The British Museum, the College of Arms and the Society of Antiquaries between them possess the finest collection of Heraldic Rolls of Arms and manuscripts in the world.

ROYAL ARMS IN CHURCHES

The Royal Arms under this heading are for the most part carved in wood and are in a number of cases coloured. Many were carved at the Restoration of the Monarchy, but only very few were carved after Queen Anne's reign.

King's College Chapel, Cambridge	Henry VII
St. George's Chapel, Windsor	Henry VIII
Elton, Herefordshire	Queen Elizabeth
Basingstoke, Hants.	James I
Abbey Dore, Herefordshire	Charles I
Wells, Somerset, St. Cuthbert's	Charles I and Charles II
Taunton, Somerset, St. Mary Magdalen	Charles II
Lydiard Tregoze, Wilts.	,,
Bristol, St. Mark's	,,
Monnington, Herefordshire	,,
London, St. Margaret Lothbury	,,
London, St. Margaret Pattens	,,
London, St. Mary at Hill	,,
London, St. Benet Paul's Wharf	,,

Twickenham, All Hallows (removed from Lombard Street, 1940)	Charles II
London, St. Paul's Cathedral	William and Mary
Lockington, Leics.	Queen Anne
Weston-under-Lizard, Staffs.	Queen Anne
Bath, Somerset, St. Mark's	George III
London, St. Ethelred's, Ely Place	Queen Victoria
Edinburgh, St. Giles' Cathedral, Chapel of the Thistle	George V
London, Queen's Chapel of the Savoy	George VI

BUILDING EXTERIORS

St. George's Chapel, Windsor	Royal Badges on walls, 15th century
St. George's Chapel, Windsor	King's Beasts on roof, 1927–30
Hampton Court Gatehouse	Arms of Wolsey, 1521
Hampton Court Moat Bridge	King's Beasts, 1909
Hampton Court, Doorway to Chapel	Royal Arms, Henry VIII, 16th century
St. Martin's in the Fields	Royal Arms, George I, 1727
Buckingham Palace	Royal Arms, George V and Queen Mary, 1913
St. Dunstan's in the West, Fleet Street, London	Royal Arms, William IV
Canterbury Cathedral Cloisters	840 coloured shields mainly 15th century
Canterbury Cathedral Gateway,	Coloured shields of arms, 15th century
Lincoln's Inn Gateway Chancery Lane, London	16th century shields
St. John's Priory Gatehouse, Clerkenwell, London	Royal Arms—Modern, 1893
St. Bartholomew the Great, Gatehouse, London	20th-century modern shields
College of Arms, London	19th-century modern shields and badges

Glastonbury, George Inn	15th-century armorial panel
Peterborough Deanery Gateway	Arms and badges, 1497–1526
Kirkham Priory Gatehouse	Shields of arms, 1289
Fotheringay Church	Falcon Badge on weathervane, 1435
Farleigh Hungerford Castle Gatehouse, Somerset	15th-century shields
Montacute House, Somerset	16th-century achievement over doorway
Oxford, Oriel College Gateway	Vaulting bosses, 1620
Oxford, Corpus Christi College	Arms on Sundial, 1581
Oxford, Bodleian Library	Door to School Quadrangle, 1613
Oxford, Merton College Gatehouse	Roof bosses, 1500
Oxford, Exeter College Gatehouse	Roof bosses, 1700
Oxford, St. John's College, Canterbury Quadrangle	Shields of arms, 1631
Oxford, University College Gatehouse	Roof bosses, 1635
Oxford, Christ Church, Tom Tower Gateway	Roof bosses, 1681
Cambridge, Trinity College Main Gate	Achievement, 15th century, Henry VIII
Cambridge, King's College Gatehouse	15th-century shield and badges
Cambridge, King's College Chapel Buttresses	Royal Badges, 15th century
Cambridge, Christ's College Gatehouse	Beaufort Arms and badges, 16th century
Cambridge, St. John's College Gatehouse	Beaufort Arms and badges, 16th century
London, Bank of England	Lions on bronze doors in Princes Street, 20th century
Edinburgh, Palace of Holyrood-house	Panel of arms
Edinburgh Castle	Modern shields of arms

BUILDING INTERIORS

London.

Westminster Abbey	Henry VII's Chapel—bronze doors, 16th century
Westminster Abbey	Nave arcading — shields of arms, 13th century
Westminster Hall	Roof (14th century) carved figures holding shields and modern Royal beasts on steps
Houses of Parliament	Victorian Grand staircase and shields. Central Hall — shields. Lord's Chamber—Royal Thrones
Queen's Chapel of the Savoy	Victorian painted arms on ceiling
Middle Temple Hall	Plasterwork ceiling — Royal arms, 1950
College of Arms	Earl Marshal's throne, arms of Queen Anne
Hampton Court	Great Hall, arms in roof, Henry VIII

Provinces

Windsor Castle	St. George's Chapel — roof bosses, Henry VIII
Windsor Castle	St. George's Hall—shields of arms, modern
Oxford, Bodleian Library	Library ceiling shields, 1612
Oxford, Bodleian Library	Divinity School vaulting shields, 1480
Oxford, All Souls College	Fireplace, S.E. Range, 1600
Oxford, All Souls College	Library plasterwork ceiling, 1598
Oxford, New College	Warden's Study — Fireplace, 1600
Oxford, New College	Dining Hall, carved panels, 16th century

Oxford, Corpus Christi Library	Plasterwork pediment, 1604
Oxford, Corpus Christi	Room over gate—overmantel 16th century
Oxford, Magdalen College Dining Hall	16th-century panelling
Cambridge, King's College Chapel	Wall arcading, shields and badges, 15–16th century
Cambridge, King's College Chapel	Choir stalls. Achievements of arms
Chiddingstone Church, Kent	Hatchments, 1645–1852
Harefield Church, Middlesex	Hatchments
Witherslack Church, Westmorland	Hatchments of Dean Barwick 1664
Sizergh Castle, Westmorland	Carved overmantels, 16th century
Levens Castle, Westmorland	Plasterwork and carved overmantels, 16th century
Edinburgh Castle, Queen Mary's Room	Painted Royal Arms, 16th century
Edinburgh, St. Giles' Cathedral	Pillars of nave—vault bosses, shields of arms, 14th–15th century

TOMBS

Canterbury Cathedral	Black Prince, 1376
Westminster Abbey	Henry VII, 1511
Westminster Abbey	Edward III, 1377
Westminster Abbey	John of Eltham, 1366
Westminster Abbey	Aymer de Valence, 1324
Beverley Minster, York	Lady Eleanor Percy, 1340
Salisbury Cathedral	William Longspee, 1226
Salisbury Cathedral	Edward Seymour, 16th century
St. George's Chapel, Windsor	George V, 1946
Worcester Cathedral	Prince Arthur, 1501
Skipton Parish Church, Yorks.	3rd Earl of Cumberland, 16th century

Framlingham Parish Church, Suffolk	Lord Surrey, 1559
Framlingham Parish Church, Suffolk	Duke of Richmond, 1529
Harefield Parish Church, Middlesex	Countess of Derby, 1636
Langar Parish Church, Notts.	Lord and Lady Scrope, 1609
Ashby de la Zouche, Leics.	2nd Earl of Huntingdon, 1561
Newland, Glos., Parish Church	Robert Greyndower (Miner), 1443
Tring, Herts., Parish Church	Sir Wm. Gore (Lord Mayor of London), 1700
Warwick, St. Mary's	Earl of Warwick, 1457
St. Alban's Cathedral	Humphrey, Duke of Gloucester, 1450
Abergavenny Parish Church	Eva de Cantelupe, 1270
Great Durnford, Wilts.	Edward Younge (Brass), 1607
Chichester Cathedral	Countess of Arundel, 1270
Bristol Cathedral	Berkeley Tombs, 14th century
Wells Cathedral	Dean Gunthorpe, 1498
Lanercost Priory, Lancs.	Dacres, 1526
Bowden Parish Church, Cheshire	Sixty quarterings on one shield, 1727
Penshurst, Kent	16th-century "Sidney" tombs
Hever, Kent	Brass, the finest in Kent, to Sir Thomas Bullen (Anne Boleyn's father), 1538
Boxgrove Priory, Sussex	Thos. de la Warr, 1554
Evelane Church, Oxon.	Duchess de la Pole, 1461
Kingston on Soar, Notts.	Sir Thos. Babington, 1547
Enfield Church, Middlesex	Joyce, Lady Tiptoft, 1446
Appleby Church, Westmorland	Anne, Countess of Pembroke, 1675–6
St. Helen's, Bishopsgate, London	Sir Thos. Gresham, 1579

STAINED GLASS

Westminster Abbey Chapter House	Modern
Westminster Abbey, Henry VII Chapel	Battle of Britain window. Modern Squadron badges.
All Hallows by the Tower	Royal Arms and others, modern, connected with Toc H.
Queen's Chapel of the Savoy	Modern Royal Arms
Gray's Inn Hall	Modern and old
Lincoln's Inn Hall	Modern and old
Middle Temple Hall	Modern and old
Liverpool Cathedral	Modern
Public Record Office, Chapel of the Rolls	Modern and old
St. George's Chapel, Windsor	Modern and old
Winchester Cathedral	Modern
Canterbury Cathedral, Chapter House	Modern
Oxford, Merton College	East window of chapel—old
Oxford, Queen's College Chapel	Old
Stoke D'Abernon Church	Old
Salisbury Cathedral	West window—old
St. Alban's Cathedral	Old
Oxford Cathedral	Old
Wells Cathedral	Old
Bristol Cathedral	Old
Gloucester Cathedral	Old
Hereford Cathedral (Audley Chapel)	Old
Windermere Church—east window	Old
Greenford Church, Middlesex	Old
Selling Church, Kent	Old
Shalford Church, Essex	Old
Stambourne Church, Essex	Old

Stamford (St. Martin's), Lincs.	Old
Fulham Palace, London	Old
Lambeth Palace, London	Old
Apothecaries Hall, London	Old
Montacute House, Somerset	Old
Ockholt Hall	Old
Penshurst Church, Kent	Old

INN SIGNS

There has of late been a revival in the Brewing Industry of the art of Inn Sign painting, and whilst here and there are some excellent designs, there is still room for improvement.

London Area—Modern.

Brunswick Arms	Old Kent Road, S.E.1
Oxford and Cambridge	New Oxford Street, W.C.
Tankerville Arms	Hounslow
Duke of Clarence	Holland Park Avenue, W.

Provinces—Modern.

The Chequers	Tonbridge, Kent
The White Hart	Bromley, Kent
The Duke of York	Cranbrook, Kent
The White Hart	Witley, Surrey
Prince of Wales	Markstey
Griffin	Danbury
Tabard	Gloucester
Bedford Arms	Woburn, Beds.
Grafton Arms	Barnham, Suffolk
Swan Arms	Denham, Bucks.
Leicester Arms	Penshurst, Kent
Lygon Arms	Broadway, Worcs.
Crosskeys Hotel	Canonbie, Dumfries

London Area—Ancient.

King's Arms, Kings Street, Southwark.
  (Arms of George III removed from London Bridge.)
Guildhall Museum—various inn signs from old London inns.

Provinces—Ancient.

The Swan, Clare, Suffolk	15th century
The George, Glastonbury, Somerset	15th century
The Rose and Crown, Tonbridge, Kent	18th century
The Royal Mount Ephraim Hotel, Tunbridge Wells, Kent	18th century

SEALS

The Great Seals of the Realm	British Museum, London.
Seals of the Barons letter, 1301	Public Record Office Museum, London.
Seals attached to Royal Charters and documents, 1095–1820	Public Record Office Museum, London.

THE HERALDRY SOCIETY

FOR those who wish to pursue Heraldry as a hobby, the Heraldry Society, East Knoyle, Wiltshire, offers excellent facilities. There is an Associate Membership for students and those under twenty-one years of age.

BIBLIOGRAPHY

Froissart's Chronicles, 13th century (Dent), 1930.

The Institution of the Most Noble Order of the Garter, Elias Ashmole, Windsor Herald, 1672.

A Display of Heraldry, John Guillim, 1679.

Historical Memorials of Canterbury, Arthur Stanley, D.D. (Dent), 1854.

Historical Memorials of Westminster Abbey, Arthur Stanley, D.D. (John Murray), 1868.

A Manual of Heraldry, Chas. Boutell, M.A. (Winsor & Newton), 1863.

Heraldry in Relation to Scottish History and Art, Sir James Balfour Paul, Lord Lyon (David Douglas), 1900.

Stall Plates of the Knights of the Order of the Garter, W. H. St. John Hope, M.A., F.S.A. (Constable), 1901.

Some Feudal Coats of Arms, Joseph Foster (Jas. Parker), 1902.

Banners, Standards and Badges from MSS. in the College of Arms (De Walden Library), 1904.

The Ancestor, Vols. 1–12 (Constable), 1901–3.

Art of Heraldry, A. C. Fox-Davies (T. C. Jack), 1904.

Heraldry as Art, G. W. Eve (Batsford), 1907.

The Most Honourable Order of the Bath, Jocelyn Perkins, M.A. (Pitman), 1913.

The Leopards of England, Rev. E. E. Dorling, M.A. (Constable), 1913.

The Order of the Hospital of St. John of Jerusalem, H. W. Fincham (Collingridge), 1915.

The Bearing of Coat Armour by Ladies, Chas. A. H. Franklyn (John Murray), 1923.

Armorial Families, A. C. Fox-Davies (Hurst & Blackett), 1929.

Complete Guide to Heraldry, A. C. Fox-Davies (Nelson), 1929.

Heraldry for Craftsmen and Designers, W. H. St. John Hope, Litt.D., D.C.L. (Pitman), 1929.

Scots Heraldry, Sir Thomas Innes of Learney (Lord Lyon) (Oliver and Boyd), 1934.

The Manual of Flags, Revised by V. Wheeler Holohan (A. Warne), 1933.

Annual Reports of The Friends of St. George's Chapel, Windsor Castle, 1934–51.

Heralds' Exhibition Catalogue (College of Arms), 1934.

The Knights of the Garter 1348–1939, Edmund H. Fellowes, M.V.O., M.A., Mus. Doc. (S.P.C.K.).

The Historic Heraldry of Britain, Anthony Wagner, F.S.A., Richmond Herald (Oxford University Press), 1939.

The Romance of St. George's Chapel, Harry W. Blackburn, D.S.O., D.C., Canon of Windsor (Raphael Tuck), 1947.

The Heraldry of Canterbury Cathedral, Commander A. W. B. Messenger, F.S.A., L.R.I.B.A. (Friends of Canterbury Cathedral), 1947.

The Colour of Chivalry, Harold Pereira (Imperial Chemical Industries), 1950.

Intelligible Heraldry, Sir Christopher and Adrian Lynch-Robinson (Macdonald), 1948.

Boutell's Heraldry, completely revised by C. W. Scott-Giles, M.A. (A. Warne), 1950.

Volumes of the Royal Commission on Ancient Monuments (H.M.S.O.).

The Coat of Arms (Quarterly Journal of the Heraldry Society), 1950.

Debrett's Peerage, Baronetage, Knightage and Companionage (Odhams).